CONVERSATIONS WITH A TREE

by
Jane Warren Campbell

Copyright © 2013, 2018 by Rashana (aka. Jane Warren Campbell) First Edition published in Canada by Inner Nature Publishing, Bear River, NS.

All rights reserved. No part of this publication may be reproduced, distributed, or transmitted in any form or by any means, including photocopying, recording, or other electronic or mechanical methods, without the prior written permission of the copyright holder.

Revised Edition (2018) Published in Canada by Into Nature Publishing, Victoria, BC

To order visit www.conversationswithatree.com

10% of all profits are donated to organizations that preserve, plant and protect trees. To inquire or register your organization, email: **info@conversationswithatree.com**

*This book is dedicated to all who have

the courage to step out of

the busyness of life and back into

the stillness of nature.*

Table of Contents

INTRODUCTION 7

Poem - *Life is Precious* 12
CHAPTER ONE
Talking to Trees – It's All About Love 13

Poem - *From Mother Earth* 46
CHAPTER TWO
From Despair to Discovery 47

Poem - *We Are One* 70
CHAPTER THREE
What? Plants Can Read my Mind?? 71

Poem - *The Visit* 96
CHAPTER FOUR
Feeling Sick? How About a Hike 97

Poem - *Blessed Be* 118
CHAPTER FIVE
Our Teachers the Trees 119

Poem - *A New Dawn* 138
CHAPTER SIX
The How and Why of Tree Talking 139

Poem - *Be a Beacon* 164
CHAPTER SEVEN
New Humans on a New Earth 165

Correspondence 192

Acknowledgments 193

About the Author 194

References 195

INTRODUCTION

This book is an invitation back to love – the love of the Divine reflected through nature. It is full of joy and wonder and grace, and the many challenges and changes that led me there. As crazy as it may sound, the greatest love I have ever experienced in this world has come from the trees. They love unconditionally. When I am with them I feel like I am truly home – home to my own true nature as Love Existing.

I've always had a deep reverence and appreciation for nature. As a teenager I would often go to the forest trail behind our house and talk to the trees. Somehow, they offered comfort as I struggled through challenging times. Of course, I never expected, or even dreamed, that one day the trees would talk to me! My communication with the them expanded decades later, at a time when I was, once again, going through a major life transition. All that had created security for me had been ripped away, leaving me vulnerable and raw. Just as I did in my teens, I retreated to nature for solace and comfort. Being in the forest helped clear my mind of all the turmoil and troubles I was facing. There were times when my nature retreat lifted me out of my mundane state of being into a whole new experience, as I felt elevated and more expansive in my awareness. And yet, I had no idea that this would lead to conversations with a tree. That's because it never occurred to me that a tree could actually communicate.

All that changed one day, while sitting at the base of a tall hemlock. Something extraordinary happened. I clearly sensed an invitation to be a scribe for the tree. I knew instantly that this tree wanted me to record its wisdom and share it with the world. Perhaps this hemlock knew that I was someone with the open mind to listen and the heart to proceed with the request to be her scribe. As I sat on the exposed root of that hemlock, there was no question that I was about to embark on an incredible journey. What I didn't know was the depth of the communications I would receive, and the loving support that the trees have to offer.

Henrietta, as my tree friend invited me to call her, guided me through my time of transformation with messages full of wisdom and grace. I was amazed at the intelligence coming through. I couldn't help but wonder how a tree could possibly know so much. I guess the real question is how could a tree possibly *know* anything!? Thankfully I believe in possibilities that lie outside of our 'normal' experience and trust my intuition to guide me in life. My interaction with Henrietta supported my understanding that there is so much about existence itself that we just don't know. It is only in hindsight that I realize the extent of energetic support I received from this tree as I made my daily trek to the grove. I found myself experiencing first-hand a connection with the oneness of nature. I would feel my cells morphing to become part of the environment - the tree, the grass and all that surrounded me. It is clear to me now that Henrietta guided me into that experience. Trees are aware of our plight as humans, disconnected from ourselves, from each other, and from our environment. They are patiently waiting for us to remember who we are, ready to offer their support as we discover our innate wisdom and our connection with the oneness of all life.

As I write this, I realize that there are many who are not ready to accept that talking to a tree is possible. It is pushing the parameters of what most would accept as reality. And yet, quantum physics, and now quantum biology, are expanding our understanding of the nature of existence. We are learning that plants have what some scientists call intelligence, and memory.

The more we keep our hearts and minds open, the more we can accept new discoveries as they arise. As we learn to trust our intuitive senses, a whole new world of possibility reveals itself. For those who feel a deep connection with nature, this book is an invitation back to love – the love of the Divine reflected through nature. There is profound wisdom and healing waiting for us in the realm of nature. Because I believe that it is possible to communicate intuitively with trees, I am able to collect this wisdom. It is a skill that we all possess. I do not have magical powers. You can do this too. You can connect to a tree by greeting it with an open heart, sending love and appreciation for its beauty and its Being. You can ask the tree what it would like to share with you and listen with your heart for the answer. With the desire to know life from a greater perspective than the logical mind perceives, many things are possible.

As my 'relationship' with Henrietta developed, I came to understand that the trees guide us in ways that most are unaware of. They offer insight to our problems, and solace in a hectic world. And though they do not need our attention or recognition, they are happy for it. Their greatest message is for us to return to love – to our own true nature through nature. My hope is that you will feel that love as you journey through this book, and the wisdom in their messages will resonate as truth for you, revealing simple solutions to the diverse problems we face in the world today.

Within these pages you will discover that a very real, yet unseen, existence awaits. It is a place where anything is possible and it's available to all who have the desire to expand into their true potential. *Conversations with a Tree* is written for all who are ready to live in a new world – a world where we remember our connection to nature and honour all of creation. It is an invitation for a new culture on Earth – one based in love. I have been touched, deep within my soul, with the love that the trees have to share. The essence of that love is captured in this book as it emanates from the messages I received in our conversations. As you journey through these pages, may your heart awaken to a greater understanding of the wisdom of nature. Conversations with a tree is really just the beginning. We are magnificent Beings, capable of tapping into a source of infinite knowing, just as the trees do. The more we return to our own true nature through nature, the more we will realize our connection to all Life. The more we realize our connection to all Life, the more we will honour our truth as Love Existing.

Teaching Moments

Have you ever read a book that left you wondering how the author accomplished what they were describing? I have. Many times, when reading a book, I would be left wondering, "How did you do that?", wishing the author had shared more detail of what they were describing. It is for that reason that I have added Teaching Moments at the end of the chapters where I felt there was something I could expand on. The Teachings may clarify some of the messages from the trees that seem very simple, yet can hold a deeper wisdom. Or, they may explain, as best I can, some skill that was mentioned in the chapter that I feel you may have questions about.

If, after reading the Teaching Moments, you still have questions, you may submit them by emailing info@conversationswithatree.com and, time permitting, I will post the answer on the website.

www.conversationswithatree.com.

On the website you may sign up to the email list to receive our monthly newsletter. You will learn about upcoming events, and every month you will receive a new message from the trees. When a question about the book is answered it will be published in the newsletter so everyone can benefit from the answers. The more we know, the more empowered we are to be living fully in our own connection to the All That Is.

If you have no need for expansion or clarification of the chapter content you can pass over the Teaching Moments and move directly to the next chapter.

Life is Precious

Oh Dear Brethren, as you walk upon this land
Do you not feel the responsibility
That lies beneath each step?

We are one with the land.
Each breath is sourced from the Earth.
Your disease is an extension
Of your ill-intent.

Free yourself from your pain.
Connect again with the source of your life.
Be kind to your Earthly mother.
Send her your love every day.
Feel gratitude for the privilege
To walk upon her shores at this time,
For life is precious.

Find the sacredness in your existence
So that we may flourish.

CHAPTER ONE

Talking to Trees – It's All About Love

Every January 6th I celebrate my birthday which, in itself, is nothing extraordinary. However, a birthday so early in the year is like a double beginning. There are all the changes and resolutions that we think about when a new calendar year approaches as well as the changing energy and numerology that a new personal year brings. Add to that the determination that my 56th year was going to be one of healing and you have a formula for change! I was ready for life to be full and rich and I knew the only way to get there was to come face to face with my wounds. At the time, I was living in a small city working at a job that was completely out of resonance with who I am. The environment was emotionally toxic to my sensitive soul. Every day I prayed to be out of there and the universe provided. On January 23rd I arrived for work at 8:30 in the morning and was gone half an hour later! I'll never forget it. It was the first day of the Chinese Year of the Dragon – another new beginning! I was 'released' from the job that I hated. Of course, I was surprised at this totally unexpected turn of events, but I connected with the blessing of it almost immediately. I went home and did my happy dance, knowing that my prayers had been answered, even though the outcome was definitely not what I had expected.

I was proud of the way I handled that experience. My new mantra was 'all change leads to something better' and I was doing a good job of trusting that. Then, about six weeks after losing my job, I learned that my landlord was selling the condo I was living in and I had to move. This time my mind immediately went into the past and directly to fear. It brought up a series of challenges, just two years earlier, that also started in January. It was definitely not an outcome that I wanted to repeat. The words of a friend, reflecting on my experience two years previous, came flashing into my mind. "When we enter into something out of fear, the outcome will reflect that fear." I had not considered that before. It reminded me of something I learned in my hypnotherapy training that really stood out for me. Basically, there are two ways of being in the world; we are either running from what we don't want or moving toward what we do want. I was saddened to realize that my life was spent 'running from' instead of 'striving toward'. Enough of that! This time I was determined to stay in a place of trust instead of dropping into the 'why me?' I chose to believe that Spirit was providing opportunities and not hardship. My new positive mindset quickly led me to realize that with no job holding me in the city, and no lease, I was free to live wherever I wanted.

It is so interesting the way things work when we are in the flow of life, or perhaps I should say when we recognize the flow of life. Just two days before my notification of the move, I had the thought that I wanted to live away from the city and be more connected to nature. Never would I have expected that the opportunity would arrive so quickly. However, with my new mindset that life was indeed supporting me, I immediately knew where my new home would be. About an hour from the city is a small community that I have always loved. It is a university town situated on the Bay of Fundy in Nova Scotia. There I would be closer to nature and closer to family. By June 1st I was moving into my new apartment and, for the first time in my life, I felt like I was truly home. There were trees and birds outside my window and one of the most beautiful views I have ever seen from the main street of town.

Every day I would make the short walk downtown and wander along the dykes. From there I could see the magnificent Cape Blomidon, a large bluff jutting into the Bay of Fundy that rises 600 feet out of the water, contributing to one of the strongest tidal currents in the world. It is stunningly beautiful. I found myself in complete awe at the shift I was experiencing in my life and the beauty that was nourishing my soul. I had definitely found my nature connection and my spirit was soaring. As I began to explore more of my new home town I discovered a trail that offered a different nature environment than the open spaces of the dyke. The small, wooded path leading to the trail is barely visible from the street. As I entered into the canopy of trees I immediately felt the serenity of the forest embrace me. The lush, green pathway, accompanied by a small, babbling brook, reminded me of the forest sanctuary that had brought me so much solace in my teenage years. The sweet sound of the water sang to my heart as I danced in delight for this new-found treasure.

The trail took me to a small pond surrounded by a grove of hemlock trees. There was something intriguing, magical almost, about the area of the pond. On the far side, a small bridge spanned the brook as it spilled out of the pond. As I crossed the tiny bridge I found myself face to face with one of the stately hemlocks, with the trail dividing on either side of it. At the base of the tree is a large, exposed root, offering a convenient spot to sit and admire the pond and soak up the scenery of the small forest. This new trail became one of my favourite places to be as I settled into my new home town.

One day, after a few visits to the trail, I stopped to give more attention to the beautiful hemlock before passing by. I put my hands on its trunk for a few moments, observing the patterns and structure of the coarse bark under my fingers. Then I stood with my back against the large trunk as I often like to do, sending my love and admiration, before taking a seat at its base. That was when the magical journey of conversations with a tree began! As I sat on the root of the tree I 'sensed' an invitation into conversation. I simply had the feeling that the tree wanted to talk to me. She asked me to buy a journal and be her scribe. Because of my experience of being a channeler, and connecting with unseen forces, I easily accepted that such a thing would be possible. After all, our sense of 'reality' is constantly changing as science, and now quantum physics, expands our awareness of existence beyond the visible third dimensional realm. The tree told me she would like to be called Henrietta, after a young woman who used to sit at her base 100 years ago, lamenting lost loves. I sensed a vision of all the people who had passed by and sat at her base over the last century. Some acknowledged her and felt her presence, and many more simply wandered by, lost in their own thoughts or the intent of their walk. I, on the other hand, was eager to hear what kind of message would come from a tree. The very next day I returned, after buying a lovely new journal to honour her request. As I sat, pen in hand, looking out over the pond with the sunlight dancing on the water, I had no idea of the significance it would have on my journey forward. It was the beginning of one of the most loving connections of my life.

As the conversations with Henrietta evolved, so did the wisdom in the information that was being received. I was immersed into a mystery that no doubt our ancestors knew and many of the shamans of today still connect to. It is beyond the norms of our every-day reality and yet, once accepted, perhaps more real than our mundane existence. Henrietta quickly proved that she has great wisdom to share and my frequent visits to her became the highlight of my day. Every time I entered the trail I was nourished by the sounds of the brook, and the birds, and the small creatures that shared the woods. Sometimes, as I sat at Henrietta's side, journal in hand, others would pass by and give a quick smile or say "hello". I was amused as I wondered what they were thinking, having no idea that my journal did not contain the usual 'Dear Diary' content. To the contrary, Henrietta was becoming a teacher – a sage – and the more I visited, the more the 'relationship' developed.

As Henrietta came to feel like a friend, I approached her one day, greeting her like I would any friend. I asked, "How are you Henrietta?" This was her response:

Asking a tree, 'How are you?' is a silly question. We have only one way of being and that is being. We do not have good days and bad days. We are. We exist. That is it. We witness that which is unfolding around us. We are aware of the noise of the saw and see that home repairs are happening close by. We notice a person walk by and observe their thoughts and emotions as they pass. We soak up the sunlight and feel the synthesis within our cells. This is our existence. Because we do not move, we cannot run away from what is as humans do. If someone approaches us with saw in hand, we realize that we are about to serve the Earth in a different way - perhaps as fire wood to warm the hearts of those who gather round the stove. They are warmed by our embers with no thanks for what we have offered. It is not that we need the thanks, for we are happy to serve in whatever way Creation brings to us. But mankind would do well to have appreciation - for its own evolution - its own connection to the All That Is. It is the loss of this connection that is a great part of the demise of humanity.

For you see, we are part of the Creator itself, as are you. We are part of the natural world that holds the core essence of the creative force of God, or All That Is. By connecting with us you are connecting with the origins of your soul. And so, as humans consume that which is derived from the natural world, it would serve them well to consider their good fortune in having this natural product to consume. Humanity, in its evolution away from the Light, has allowed itself to become very disconnected from the essence of nature. In its place is a yearning but no true understanding of what one is yearning for. The quest for connection has led to addictions. The empty soul seeks pleasure through lust, alcohol, drugs, TV. The list goes on. And it goes on because soul satisfaction does not come from these things. The deep yearning is for your true nature - your nature as humans connected to the Divine.

We are here to serve you. It is our greatest pleasure to support you in whatever way we can. Thankfully for us, the trees, we have our connection to Mother Earth. She sustains us as we do her. She appreciates what we offer to her carefully planned ecosystems. She is the great Mother - always looking to improve and grow spiritually so that she can lead her 'children' to ever greater heights. And so, as we reach into the heavens, we are also deeply anchored into the Earth. Our roots spread to embrace our Mother Earth and our branches reach up to give praise to our Father Sun. We are balance on this Earth. Those who are in the cities are lost to this way of being. Therefore, it is those who live among us (the trees) who will be the first to see the way out of darkness. It is those who appreciate the beauty around them who also reflect that beauty from their hearts. They are the ones who will lead all of humanity out of the darkness.

And so, as you sit at my base, remember these words. Life is precious. It can pass in a fleeting moment. Is it worth the headache and heartache that is your current way of being? Those who have stepped out of the rat race know the difference. Those who have stepped away from materialism are finding their way back to their hearts. It is not a big mystery. It is surrender. Surrender your life to simplicity. Stop running. Anchor yourself into the Earth. Then your heart will be filled with joy. As you honor the Earth and her creations you will be honoring yourself. In honoring yourself in this way you will feel the wholeness of life begin to bubble up in your essence. The deep yearning and emptiness will be replaced by fulfillment and wonder. Sadness will fall away to joy as you remember your true essence. This awaits you but you must make the choice. You can let the idea of having to sacrifice your current life keep you from this choice or you can realize that the only life worth living awaits you and moving toward it is not sacrifice but wisdom.

We are deeply delighted with the opportunity to share this knowledge with you today.

For a brief moment, I was a little taken aback to be called silly, especially by a tree! However, I was quickly pulled into the message and the depth of her words. What she spoke resonated as deep truth for me. I was certainly experiencing the shift from city living to being closer to the land. I was happier than I had been in decades.

Years before my experience of communicating with the trees I remember reading two different books that described, in great detail, living more connected to the land. One was about a tribal type of living, where all life was honoured. The people would connect telepathically with the animals that they needed to kill for food, asking for one to sacrifice itself. They lived simple, joy-filled lives, at one with all. As I read about such an existence I found myself yearning for the same. In comparison to how we currently live on this Earth, it seemed that all we give importance to –

money, prestige, a narrow version of beauty, busyness, competition – was insignificant. In its place was a connection to one another, to the land and to all of existence. Now the trees were telling me that we are on our way back to something similar. The basis of what they share is that we are finding our way out of the fear that has us so stressed and suppressed and back to a life that exists more fully from the foundation of love. The mere thought of it is comfort for my weary heart.

Henrietta shared many messages about love, and the need for us humans to find our way back to loving ourselves in order to create the heaven on Earth that we so desire. The very essence of her words often carried the energy of what I would describe as Divine love. Even as I read them years later I am moved to the depth of my heart by what she has to say. Because of the love I felt from Henrietta I was inspired to ask, "What can a tree tell humans about love?" There is so much wisdom in her answer:

We can tell you what true love feels like. There is no judgement – ever! Love does not judge, it accepts. A tree knows that love because it does not have the mind that creates scenarios that are out of harmony with the truth. A tree knows love as the essence of life – the light from the sun and the nourishment from the Earth. The mere sustenance of life is a gift of love. Knowing that everything we need to survive is provided to us is love. This is true for humans as well but you have lost that understanding. You have forgotten that all your needs are provided for. You have forgotten to appreciate the sun for the life it brings and to thank your Earthly mother for the land beneath your feet. You have forgotten that the song birds sing for your delight. You have forgotten that the flowers bloom to appeal to your senses. We, the trees, have not forgotten, for it is all we have. We are not distracted by the need for creation other than growing and sustaining ourselves. Therefore, we do not see anything but what is. Sometimes we see love in people and sometimes we see fear covering up that love.

Trees are kind to one another. We will grow where we are planted. If two seedlings start life side by side they will share the soil and the sunlight and they may grow into tall stately trees, side by side, sharing and existing together. Do they feel each other? Oh yes, they do and they come to appreciate their existence in that way. They learn to live harmoniously. When they have completed their cycle on the Earth and one falls, it may take the other down with it. There will be nothing but total acceptance of that. There are no conditions of existence as a tree, other than the environment. Love is easy for a tree. As the trees take their sustenance from the Earth and the sky, they also draw prana from the ethers and they offer it back to the Earth. This is love. Prana is love. Chi, energy, it is all love. The very force that keeps you alive is love. Have you thought of it that way? It is nothing less than love. So, the mere fact that you are here walking the Earth is love. You are so removed from that now that you have forgotten. We, the trees, are happy to remind you, for this realization can change your life if you allow it. If you give it enough of your attention you will be changed. You breathe love. You walk love. You exist — love in action. That is what you are at the core.

How you think you could live without love is merely a reflection of your forgetting. As you go about your day remember that the energy that keeps you moving is love. As you breathe, remember that you are breathing love. And where did the air for your breath come from? It has passed through the trunks of trees. It has moved through the lungs of lovers as they join in passionate joy. It has nourished a newborn babe taking its first breath. This is the wonder of life. It is all shared. You are not alone. You have breathed the breath of someone on the other side of the world. Is this not love? It is beautiful. It is delight. It is joy. It is heaven. That of which I speak is heaven on Earth. All you have to do is remember and hold it in your awareness and you will create heaven on Earth once again. It is so simple. Humans like to complicate things, but it is so simple. Love is all there is.

Every time I read that message I have to pause to let it settle into the depths of my heart, like nothing more needs to be said…

My visits to Henrietta continued all summer long. After a while I noticed I was attracting the attention of a little squirrel. It seemed to anticipate my visits as much as I looked forward to the next beautiful message from Henrietta. I would not be there for long before it made its way across the forest to one of the branches above me. It would slowly move its way down the trunk until it was just a couple of feet above my head. There it would wait in seeming curiosity at my presence. I wondered if I was, in a sense, more at one with the forest when I was so connected to Henrietta and so in love with the surroundings. I know my heart was full – filled with gratitude for the beauty of the forest and the life I was living. When we are filled with love we vibrate at a higher frequency. I once had the experience, when working with a group of young children, of seeing a golden pillar of Light that I believe was an angel. It was like a brief flash out the corner of my eye. I knew I was able to see it because I was feeling so much love for the children in that moment that I had raised my vibration enough to connect to the higher frequency of Light that the Being existed in. Perhaps, on a lesser scale, that is why the squirrel was attracted to me when I was sitting with Henrietta.

In time, I realized that the squirrel wasn't the only observer of my visits with my new tree friend. The pond that supports the hemlock grove that Henrietta is a part of also appeared to be a breeding ground for little blue dragon flies. Actually, I believe they are damselflies. One day, as I was visiting Henrietta and fulfilling my duties as her scribe, there was a damselfly that sat on a small plant nearby. It rested there without moving like the others did. I was curious about its presence. As so often happened, Henrietta would answer my question without me even asking. She was obviously aware of all my thoughts. She told me the damselfly was recording. I didn't ask for clarification. My sense was that, for some reason, it had the job of recording the moment that Henrietta and I were experiencing. I did not feel the need to know more.

The damsel flies visited another time when I decided to connect to Henrietta from a nearby park instead of going to the trail. In the park, I could sit on a bench and relish the sight of the great variety of flowers that were carefully tended by the town gardeners. Once settled, I closed my eyes to connect with Henrietta and then opened them to see two damselflies near my leg. Then one decided to rest on my leg and sat there as I wrote. It was a tiny red one. It would leave, seemingly to catch a small insect, and then return. It did that several times. As I made contact with Henrietta she told me that the more I connect with the natural world the more it connects with me.

Having finished my conversation with Henrietta I closed my journal and, as if on cue, the damselfly returned, resting beside me on the bench. At that point, I had the thought that if nature is connecting more with me then perhaps I could connect with the damselfly. I journeyed within and was told that I had to connect to the over-soul of damselfly in a sense. As I did, a large blue damselfly came into my awareness. I asked about the meaning of the damselflies coming to me and was told that it was indeed to recognize my connection with nature. I asked about many people being attracted to dragonflies as symbols of transformation. It told me that I am transformed – like one with the natural world. As if to prove its point I had a momentary feeling of being so connected to the nature around me that my cells were morphing and blending with my surroundings – as if there was no distinction between me and the environment. I was one with it all. It was very cool! I had just experienced one of those very brief, indescribable moments of being pulled into a different dimension. When I asked about the role of dragonflies I got the sense, similar to Henrietta and the trees, that it is to be. Very simple. It also said humans would do well to notice nature instead of being lost in the busyness of the mind. It ended by saying that it was good for me to be sharing this – to help open the minds of humans to the possibility of existing in a deeper connection to nature.

In my new-found freedom, summer continued to expand into a seeming endless realm of possibility. One day, after receiving a message from Henrietta, I asked what else she would like me to share. She replied:

Do you remember when you stood before the sound healer in New York and burst into tears? She looked at you like you had lost it. But you knew what the tears were about. You knew that it was a recognition of that same gift within yourself – dormant but oh so ready to awaken. You can be that to others. They will see their Light within you and choose to shine as brightly. That is the gift of fully living in the Divine essence of who you are. Each and every one of you has this beautiful Light within. When gathered together in loving support you are the rainbow bridge that leads humanity into the new essence of who you truly are. Humanity is awakening to its God-self nature.

Then, as I walked away from her, and back over the bridge after saying good-bye, I could feel her sending me so much love and appreciation that I was moved to tears. I will never forget it. It is a love unlike what I have experienced from other people. It is pure and unconditional, similar to the love that I feel from the Guides and Higher Beings of Light that I work with. Love – straight up – with no conditions. That, I learned, is one of the greatest gifts the trees have to offer us.

Well into the summer I had a similar experience when I was offering a workshop in Toronto. Being such a nature lover, I am not fond of cities. I was also working on changing what, in the past, had been uncomfortable experiences when travelling alone. As was my focus for the year, I was determined to heal those negative memories around travelling and have a positive experience. As I was discovering, the attitude we carry into our experiences plays a large part in determining the outcome as one that is positive or negative. Even though I could feel memories of fear and discomfort in travelling alone, I had decided to turn that around. In that quest, a dear couple, whom I hardly knew at all, offered me a place to stay while I was in Toronto. Not only did they open their home to me, but I happened to get a drive from Nova Scotia to Toronto with one of them and had a very pleasant trip. This time I was being supported and not feeling alone.

To my delight, the part of the city where they lived was full of trees and flowers. It was mid-summer and everything was in full bloom. Every day, to give my hosts some space, I would go out for a walk around the neighbourhood. I was so happy to be in such a beautiful part of the city that I was expressing my gratitude to the flowers and trees as I walked by and giving thanks to the All That Is for such a favourable travelling experience this time. On two different occasions, while out on my walk, I found myself being moved to tears even though I was not feeling sad. Much the opposite. I was in deep gratitude so I didn't understand what the tears were about. The second time it happened I simply asked in my head, "What is going on?" The answer quickly came, just as it did with Henrietta. I was told that I was sending so much gratitude to the trees and flowers that they (I believe the trees in particular) were sending love back to me and that created the feeling, that unconditional love again, that was moving me to tears. I still feel blessed whenever I think of those experiences.

And so it was, my summer days passed into autumn. I felt some sadness when I noticed the trail changing as the weather turned colder. The ferns were turning brown and the days held a chill that spoke to me of a time when I would not be comfortable sitting outdoors to write at Henrietta's side. I knew I could connect with Henrietta from home, just like I could connect with my Guides without seeing them, but it created an emptiness none-the-less. It was such a glorious time visiting her so often. As if to soothe that feeling, the adventures of the summer expanded as I continued to explore the town. I had noticed a trail, close to the dyke, that travelled along adjacent to the main street of town. One day I decided to check it out to see if I was missing anything. To be honest, the trail didn't really excite me. It didn't have the same feeling as being in the woods or the incredible view overlooking Cape Blomidon. I wandered along until it reached a residential neighbourhood and then turned around to walk home.

On the way back a particular tree caught my attention. It was tall compared to the other more shrub-like trees around it. It was part of a narrow divide of trees, roses, and other bushes between the trail and the open field that led to the dyke. It was a fir or spruce of some type, the kind with long, hanging fronds from the branches. I had the distinct feeling that it called out to me and that is why I stopped. It hadn't caught my attention at all when I passed by the first time. I stood there, making a connection, and it immediately introduced itself as George – en francais if you will! As I connected with him I was intrigued. Although identifying as male, George had a much softer energy than Henrietta. He felt very nurturing and gentle whereas Henrietta's energy was more matter of fact. Of course, I was going to take full advantage of this opportunity to communicate with another tree. Even though the environment was almost uninviting, he was so delightful that I had to return. A couple of days later I went back with my journal, wondering if we could have the same connection I had with Henrietta, and intrigued to find out what he would have to say. I was not disappointed. Some of his messages go deep into the world of quantum physics, with information that challenges our outdated beliefs.

In one of my first conversations with George I asked if he could expand on the message that so often came from Henrietta about us humans finding our way back to our true nature through nature. His reply started with "A delightful question indeed…" which took me by surprise. Although I felt deep love from Henrietta, I hadn't heard her expressing herself with what I would consider an emotional response. When I asked George about this he told me that he was simply expressing his personality with words that I could relate to. The use of the word delightful certainly did reflect his personality. This is the rest of his response to my query:

A delightful question indeed for humans have stepped far from their source being the Earth and the sun. You have even been taught to be afraid of the sun. The sun is the source of all life. Without the rays of the sun falling upon this Earth you would not survive. You know this and yet you have lost your connection to it. The same goes with the Earth. You know that she provides everything you need to survive and yet, the way it is manipulated and bastardized, it is a wonder that you can survive at all. Many are finding their way back. It is becoming so obvious now that you are beginning to understand how far removed you are from the source of all life. This is a good thing. As people make choices for food that is organic and non-GMO, you are also bringing yourselves back to the natural world and developing an appreciation for mother Earth and the sun in a way that you have not had for eons of time.

New technology will be coming very soon that will see you living in a way that can honor the Earth and still have your needs met. No longer will you rape and pillage the Earth for your survival. There is technology that can support all the population of the Earth without causing her any harm whatsoever. Do not let the leaders of your countries tell you that this is not possible. It is and it already exists. Soon, with the uprisal and the demands of the people, more and more will be revealed. It will soon be safe to bring these inventions forward. It will be such a beautiful turn of events because you will be able to enjoy all the benefits of your technology and also be restoring the Earth back to her pristine beauty. As you do, you will realize that your own beauty is sourced from the Earth. You, as a human race, will begin to appreciate more of what is, instead of thinking everything must be something else. An example of this is that you will begin to appreciate aging instead of thinking everyone must look youthful. This will come from appreciating the fullness of life. As you appreciate the fullness of life, you do not have the desire for anything to be different than it is. Each person will be respected and nurtured to be just who they are, with all their quirks and personality traits being appreciated for what they are.

From this shift in thinking you will find much less violence on the Earth. Violence comes from pain and fear acting out in the physical. When the young are raised from a place of acceptance for who they are and nurtured with kindness and gentleness, then they do not have to act out anything but love when they mature and make their way in the world. All this lies before you as you find your way back to nature and your true nature. Your true nature is to be loving and kind. Right now, this is taught out of you, as you are raised in a society that compares the child to what others believe is the norm. If the child does not fit in somehow, then the child is taught to be different than its true nature in order to be accepted. This creates great pain and hardship and it is what you see around the world.

So I am delighted to speak of this and to share with you what lies ahead for you in the times that you are moving into. It is very exciting for you and for all of nature. We were on the brink of extinction. Most of you do not know that but it is true. The system almost crashed before it was rescued. And who rescued it? It was the humans who almost destroyed it. There would be no other way. That is the way of it. So, it is very beautiful to see that you have saved yourselves by saving the Earth. Now is the time of restoration. Just as it was a long cycle that led you to the brink of destruction, so will it be a long cycle to restoration. And yet, it will immediately feel like a more gracious world because you have hit bottom and you are on your way back up. Everything feels better than it did on the bottom.

It turns out that his messages had a different feeling from Henrietta's as well as his 'personality' being different. Even though Henrietta was more matter of fact, her messages were about love and finding our way back to love. George, on the other hand, felt softer but his communications were more educational – as you will read further on - even more profound than what Henrietta had shared, which is saying something!

This is how my year unfolded. Never could I have imagined that my faith that 'all change leads to something better' would direct me to such incredible experiences. Henrietta continued to support me as summer turned into fall which turned into winter. As the seasons changed, and the chill of December set into my bones, I seldom made my way onto the trail. However, one day I needed to get out of the house. It was December 18th and I was feeling very out of sorts, as if something was hanging over me, but I had no idea what. There was nothing troubling on my mind or in my life. I decided to go for a walk, hoping that getting outside might lift the heavy feeling. I knew the dyke would be cold that time of year so I bundled up and headed downtown. As I stood on the wintery shore I felt no different. For some reason, Blomidon was not offering its usual reprieve, so I headed for the trail where I would be protected from the chilling wind. As soon as I was onto the trail and among the trees I felt better. Literally, I was only a few feet onto the path when I could feel the difference. It was so tangible that I was somewhat amazed. I wandered along aimlessly, the trail very different now that the foliage had died in the undergrowth. When I made my way to Henrietta I leaned against her trunk for a few moments as I often did. While there I simply wondered to myself why I had been feeling so off kilter. Immediately Henrietta answered my unspoken question. She told me that I was picking up on the mass consciousness of fear around the December 21, 2012 date that was only three days away. If you will remember, December 21, 2012 was the end of the Mayan calendar, and many people were equating that to mean the end of the world. The fear consciousness was so massive that apparently, I was picking up on it. Fortunately, I knew that instead of being something to fear, it was a time to be celebrated as a grand beginning. Henrietta explains what we can look for in this new era:

You have asked me about humans finding their way back to their true nature and I would say to you that this is something that is changing now that you are at the time of the Precession of the Equinoxes (the name of this great cycle). *Everything on the planet and all systems are changing at this time. So, to ask of man's true nature, well that is changing as well. People must now rediscover their true nature. We see that there will be a gradual swing back to living closer to the land. People will live in smaller communities, supporting each other with food and skills. This will be a much slower and more enjoyable manner of living than is currently found in your very hectic lifestyles and highly populated community centers. This, in essence, will be finding your way back to your nature as animal. Living closer to the land is a natural state of being for all animal species. Your draw away from the land also led to a disconnect from your true selves. This included your own innate intelligence. As you moved off the land you moved out of your hearts and into the mind. When living in the mind, you lost the connection to the intuitive or more feminine aspect of being and became unbalanced in your importance given to intellectual intelligence. To be intelligent without wisdom is not always useful. It is the wisdom of the intuitive aspect of intelligence that balances what is to be accomplished with that intelligence. There are certain scientists who use their intuition in their work and they are able to make new discoveries at a much higher rate than the more cerebral members of the scientific community.*

The intuition is beginning to awaken again on Earth and so it too will be leading you back to your true nature regarding your forward progress at this time. It is the intuition that will lead you to natural cures and to the knowing that much has been kept from you. As you awaken to your own inner knowing, many secrets will be revealed, no longer able to be hidden in the energy of awareness that you are awakening into. For this reason, you will begin to manage your energy resources very differently and much will change in this regard. This is good news for your planet, for you almost drove her to extinction. When the oceans are dead the planet and all life upon her are not far behind. (As I write this there is evidence that the nuclear disaster in Japan from Fukushima is now affecting life in the Pacific Ocean. Reports state that tuna being caught are all showing signs of radioactivity!) *We would say that, just in the brink of time, have you found your way back into your hearts so that this destruction of the planet will end. There are genius solutions to all your problems on Earth – pollution and such - genius indeed. They will begin to come forward now that the secrets are being revealed and you will quickly be able to heal this planet that has suffered far too long.*

*So, as a tree, I am delighted to tell you these words and share this understanding. I can see your future as I peer into the All That Is. It is written there, so to speak. Your planet will be saved, with most of the population intact. This makes many happy, for it was the desired outcome. Gaia has protected you more than you know, in order for you to survive. For you see, planets are life forms, just like everything else. All matter comes from Love. All matter. There is no exception. And so, it is joyous that Gaia and all her inhabitants are here to live on in this new era. It is this new era that is leading you back to the truth of who you are. You will find more and more that people are open to thinking about the possibility of what they feel when they walk through the forest as opposed to walking through the mall. People will begin to awaken to that as it becomes more spoken of. It is good to be telling people that you speak to a tree. Many will ridicule you, yes. But, you will also give many, many more the permission to be honest about their relationship with trees and all of nature. It has been a bit taboo in your society so it has gone unspoken. The radicals who are willing to step into their truth are the ones that give permission to all. And it is very important now for this to be happening so that you can heal this planet and your very souls along with it. We are delighted to see this happening, for **all***

life everywhere is impacted by what is happening on this planet. *You will see in time that this is truth.*

If more people had known about this grand cycle there wouldn't have been the fear that I was picking up on that day that I felt so out of sorts. Much has been kept from us regarding this grand opportunity that we are currently living in. What the Mayan's knew, that is not every day knowledge, is that the Earth moves through a cycle, as our solar system travels through the Milky Way, that takes about 26,000 years. December 21, 2012, the last date on the Mayan calendar, was when the old cycle ended and a new one began. When you think about moving into a 26,000 year cycle, hundreds of years can pass and we will still be at the beginning of this new cycle. The trees obviously know about this because they reference our evolution many times. Every time we move into a new cycle, it is an opportunity to rise up in a sense, and enter a new vibrational level of being. Evidence of this is available, as scientists have recently discovered that the Schuman Resonance of the Earth has increased in frequency. Until very recently the Schuman Resonance was steady at 7.83 Hz for many decades. However, as we enter this new cycle, it continues to increase. Monitors at the Russian Space Observing System recently showed spikes as high as 16.5 Hz are being observed. However, a few years after the beginning of the Precession of the Equinoxes, there have been reported days where the Schuman Resonance is over 100 Hz. That is an incredible increase in the vibration of the Earth! What all this is leading to I find very exciting, as described by the trees:

We are able to see what is about to transpire and it is so delightful. The very energetic soup that you live in, as does all life on Earth, is changing. It is becoming more pure. Just like cleaning a home with fresh air in the spring, the Earth is being cleansed with new, higher vibrating energies and this is leading to great change. This is very good. The Earth would not have been able to endure much more of humanity's disrespectful actions.

We are happy to tell you that all of humanity will begin to awaken to the fullness of what it is to be human and you will come to understand that you too can communicate with trees and reach the levels of understanding where all information is stored. This is not just a special skill of one person. More and more people will begin to awaken to their own abilities and to their own intuitive knowing. It is beautiful to behold what the world is moving into. For, as you become more intuitively aware, you will know how another feels when you put them down. Once you have this understanding, and especially the understanding that it is truly yourself that you are hurting, then people will stop such acts. This will expand and expand so that, over a few short years, people will become more and more loving and the Earth will be such an easier place to live. The Earth has been a hard school and for the sensitive people, almost too hard to endure. We are happy to see that this is changing.

As part of this shift we see you returning to nature as well. We see you choosing to live your lives more in harmony with the rhythms of the environment in which you live. This will give you more of the balance that will lead to better lives, without all the stress that is killing so many of you. By choosing to walk away from the hectic lifestyles that used to sustain you, then you will become happier and come to understand that you were really kidding yourselves before about what made you happy. You will realize that many of the distractions were just that — distractions so that you would not have to truly look at your life and admit how miserable you were. Now, with embracing a slower lifestyle, you can take time to look at what is important. Money will lose its value in the sense that it will not be seen as the only source of happiness. You will come to see that those who have always lived closer to the land have not needed monetary abundance in order to be happy. When people live closer to the land they derive their quality of life from the land, and the Earth supports them in that way. This is the harmony that you have lost. Your disconnect from nature has torn your hearts away from the Earth and you feel the loneliness from that, but do not know where to go to get it back because you have not recognized the source of your loneliness. Now that you know it is your disconnect from nature, you can go back to that source to find it. You will begin to see very soon how fulfilling it is to be in nature. If you take the time to think about it, you will soon see how simple it is to get that fulfilling feeling back again. So, come talk to a tree. Hug a tree and see how you feel. You will feel us if you believe it is possible. And of course, it is.

My visit to the trail on December 18th was solid proof of what Henrietta spoke of. The shift I felt by being in the woods was immediate. Henrietta told me that the reason I felt better as soon as I entered the trail is because trees don't hold fear. They only hold love. That was the reason that I immediately felt better. It was like the trees hold such a bubble of love that, as soon as I entered that bubble, the fear energy couldn't penetrate it. I was amazed at the change in how I felt, just by being in the woods. I went from being in a funk to feeling fabulous and it was as easy as a walk in the park! It is evident to me that the trees are here to support us as part of this precious ecosystem that is the Earth. They want us to remember who we are and to restore our love of nature which will, in turn, restore our love of self. They remind us that, when we are in nature, we feel more of our authentic selves and we develop a deeper appreciation for the natural world that we are a part of. What we appreciate and love we care for, including ourselves. The more we return to nature the more we will discover this peaceful state of being once again.

When I reflect on that fateful day when I was 'released' from my job, I see the great opportunity that life is always offering us. All the nuances that were aligned for me to meet Henrietta and George were carefully placed in my path. I feel so blessed that I had the eyes to see the way, and the open heart - cracked open by circumstance - to say yes to change and possibility. The trees want us to know that we are awakening to a new existence. We are evolving, and the easiest way to integrate this change is to soften and slow down and come back to ourselves. Not surprisingly, the trees invite us into nature to find our way back, and I can attest to the benefits of doing that. They stand as sentinels of grace and acceptance, and being among them leads us back to a similar vibration within ourselves, even though we are seldom aware of it.

As I healed the past, I came to understand why the trees encourage us back to self-love. When I was not fully loving myself, I would not allow myself to receive all the riches that life had to offer. My subconscious beliefs would sabotage my efforts so I wouldn't allow my desires to become my experience. The more I healed, so I could truly love myself, the fuller life became. Often over the years I have asked to be a messenger of Love in this world. What I didn't know at the time was I had to start with loving myself. The next conversation showed me how fully I came to understand what love is as my year of healing evolved, according to Henrietta that is. My words are in bold in response to her questions to me:

What do you think love is? **"It is the unconditional appreciation for all life."** *That is a very good answer. It surprises me actually. You have a good grasp of what love is. So, we will use your words to speak of love. First you used the word unconditional. That is an important aspect of real love. There are no conditions. You do not have to behave a certain way or meet any expectations of another. Real love accepts ALL that is. So, that is a good word to use to start the definition. Then you speak of appreciation - again, a very wise choice. Appreciation does not speak of neediness, which is what many humans equate love with.*

Appreciation also has no conditions. When one is in appreciation for all life, then there is regard for all life. If you are appreciating something, you cannot be critical of it. So, if humans could find the place of appreciating everything and everyone, the world would be full of love.

What else could we say of love? **"We could say that it is acceptance."** *Yes, indeed. Acceptance is another aspect of love. This is the key to self-love, which is where all love comes from. If you accept all aspects of who you are then you will be loving yourself. When you are loving yourself, there is no need to criticize or belittle yourself or others. So, acceptance means allowing. You allow yourself to be who you are and you allow others to be who they are as well. We now have in our definition the words appreciation, acceptance, and allowing. The three As of love. We would like you to remember this and use it for positive self regard. For you see, love is the foundation to happiness. It does not come from another. It does not come from possessions. It does not come from accomplishments. It comes from the appreciation and acceptance of the self. And when you are in appreciation and acceptance of the self, then you allow the self to express honestly in the world. There is no need to put on a face of what the world wants to see. There is no need to try to be someone else, believing that you are less than perfect. There is no need to try and fit a mold. You are the mold of you. It is when you try to fit into another's perception of what your mold should be that you suffer. End the suffering by accepting that you are perfect just the way you are. Maybe you do not always behave in ways that you like, but when you start truly accepting and appreciating yourself, you will stop behaving in that way. The more you love yourself the less unlovable you become, based on society's interpretations of love. The more you love yourself, the less you have to act out - crying out for love. You have it within. Searching for love outside of the self is never successful.*

Others will always view you from their perspective and their expectations, unless they are in the three As of love themselves. Then they will see you as perfect and will not look to you to fill their empty heart space. If they are not searching outside of themselves, then they will not look to you for their awareness of love. But, if you are searching for love outside of yourself with others who are doing the same, that is the formula for suffering. They will not see the fullness of you. They cannot because they do not see it for themselves. Therefore, they will expect you to fill the emptiness that they experience and when you do not live up to those expectations, the honeymoon is over. Whereas, when your love comes from within, there is no honeymoon period. It is balanced love. It is not the highs and lows of emotion. It is the deep-seated feeling state of love. There is a difference. Only those who get glimpses of the depth of unconditional love have an awareness of what that truly feels like.

"Why are you expressing this way? It is different from your usual mode of expression."

It is because of the place where humanity is in their evolution at this time and the evolution of the Earth. Because we have passed December 21, 2012 many people have the thought that the world is not ending so they can just go about life the way they always have. This is not the truth. The world has and is still changing. In order for humanity to keep up with the evolution of the Earth, there is the need to find this love within the self. Without it, people will be living the expression of not love. And that does not feel very good. We are in a new time with new energies on the Earth. Those energies mean that more than ever man is a creator of his own life. What you create is a reflection of your love of self and what you believe you deserve. It is for this reason that we speak of love in this way today. You are a channel for this work Jane and this is why it comes through you via many different sources. It feels repetitive to you because, regardless of who you are connecting with, you seem to have this overview of messages that are all related. It is because it is your mission at this time to be delivering this message. It is your work for this year to be doing this. It is not all that you will do but it is a big part of the focus for the year. We know of your intentions to publish this work and so it is an opportunity to educate humanity about what is important in these years following the shift of the ages.

From my own healing journey, and working to support others, I have discovered the deep connection between our hidden, subconscious beliefs and the reality we create for ourselves. What many people don't realize is that all of our responses in the world come from our beliefs. We can think happy thoughts and try to turn our lives around but as long as we are not truly loving ourselves, deep inside, we will not create the life we dream of. This book begins with love because the trees want us to know that life is all about love. It's not just love that we feel in our hearts. According to the trees, love is life itself.

Can there be too much love in the world? I can't imagine why such a thing could be true. Love is all there is. Love is the reason for existence. Love is what keeps your molecules together. Without love you would just be a bunch of particles floating out in space. So, how could love ever be a topic that is spoken of too often? Indeed, it is not spoken of often enough, at least in the deeper understanding of what love truly is. For you see, love truly is the essence of all life. It is love that opens the petals of a flower. It is love that calls the humming bird to feed of its nectar. It is love that causes hunger in the wolf. It is love that heals the tears of a child. It is also love that harms the child and starves the wolf and kills the flower, you just have trouble seeing it that way.

There is love behind everything – it is just that you humans like it more when the love feels good. And yet, if you stay with your pain long enough with enough sincerity, you will find the love there. When a human can see love behind the darkness, they have mastered the human existence. And that is where many of you are headed in these times. That is where the Earth is headed. Mother Earth, in her great love for all the life forms upon her surface and below it, knows well of this. She has endured more than you truly are aware of in her service to all. On the brink of destruction, she still waits for you. She holds out for you in the hope that one more person will travel with her into the higher realms of existence. Oh, the magic in the understanding of which we speak. It is beautiful indeed.

Again, the trees offered such a beautiful message that I could read it over and over. This is a taste of what the trees have taught me about love. It is messages like the ones that I have shared with you, that led me out of hardship and despair, and assisted me in my own personal evolution into peace and contentment. However, that journey was not always easy. As the year unfolded, I still had to face the deeply hidden, limiting beliefs that I needed to heal in order to fully embrace the potential of living in a state of self-acceptance. As I write this, I realize it is symbolic of what is happening now, in the bigger picture. There is war and suffering as the old falls away. It must crumble in order for a new Earth to manifest. Just as I was determined to heal and create a new and better life for myself, humanity, as a team, must do the same as we are transformed from the ashes of the past. And just as I was loved and supported by the trees, they stand, as sentinels of love, ready to support all of humanity in the same way. In the next Chapter I share the struggle I went through as the year unfolded. It is offered as a story of hope for the evolution of humanity as we rise out of the mire that has been our way of living for centuries into the great awakening that is available to us all in these magnificent times.

Teaching Moment

Going Within

In this chapter I mentioned "going within" to be more connected Henrietta. I start by being fully present in the moment, ensuring my thoughts are not on something else. Then I feel my physical body in relation to my surroundings. Perhaps it is feeling the roots I am sitting on or the ground beneath me. I may also consciously ask that all my energy be here with me in this moment. We can easily leave parts of our energy out in the ethers you could say, leaving aspects of our awareness at the grocery store where we shopped earlier in the day or with a loved one back at home. When I consciously intend to bring all my energy into my body, I feel aspects of myself returning. Intention is powerful in anything we choose to experience. By intending that you are fully present, and then getting silent, it makes a difference.

To go within after you are centered, I shift my awareness into my heart. Literally imagine yourself dropping from your mind into your heart. Asking from this space brings a different awareness to you and, with practice, you will find that you can sense an inner voice or message. The message may come in words, images, sounds, symbols or just a feeling or a knowing. Don't dismiss what comes to you. We make our intuitive work harder than it really is. Essentially, it feels like our imagination and because of that, it is easy to ignore it. I like to say that our imagination can be more real that what we call reality.

Going within is being fully present in the moment, in your physical body and aware of your surroundings. With practice your intention will bring you there very quickly.

Once you are centered within yourself, then it is time to ask for the guidance you seek. Again, it is often easier than you may think. I know when I first started connecting with my Guides I wanted it so badly that I remained in my mind instead of my heart. It took me years to realize that I had the answers within all along. Because it can seem like imagination, it can take time to trust what is coming through. What worked for me was to share what I was receiving with others to get feedback on the validity of what I was receiving. I would invite people to ask questions through me so that I could get their feedback as to the accuracy of the answer I received.

On the other hand, if you receive nothing, pay attention during the rest of the day and the next few days, to any external signs that are responding to your question. Sometimes our Higher Essence will talk to us through others or through nature, such as seeing certain animals or birds. Everything in our experience is showing us something about ourselves. Pay attention. Become curious, and trust that what you seek is on its way. Be patient and have fun with it. For example, if you are in the middle of traffic and a humming bird flies past your window, pay attention. That's not a common place to see a humming bird. Humming bird represents joy. Look up the meaning of the animal or flower that catches your attention. The more we consciously attune to nature, the more we will learn from it. (I share a powerful nature experience later in the book that will give you a better sense of what I mean here.)

Knowing How Another Feels When You Put Them Down

I would like to expand on part of the tree message in this chapter. It stated that we are coming into a time when 'you will know how another feels when you put them down ... and it is truly yourself that you are hurting'. I once had the experience of feeling that to my core. It was one of those moments that is hard to describe because it was like, for a brief second, I was pulled into another reality and out of my 'normal' human experience. It happened many years ago. I was in a conversation with a friend and I had said something unkind about someone we were talking about. I immediately felt like I had been stabbed in the heart. Literally! It was such a powerful feeling that I even gasped. That experience left no doubt in my mind that my comment about the other person was a deep hurt toward myself. It was a brief moment of experiencing the truth like the tree had said.

Since that time, I have come to understand that experience more fully. When we speak ill of another it is truly ourselves that we are hurting because, ultimately, there is no other – there is only ourselves. This is a hard concept to grasp if it is new to you and, further along in this book, it is actually addressed in one of the tree conversations. Our experiences are created by our mind you could say, and every person in our experience is showing us something about ourselves – the mirror effect. When we criticize someone else, we are truly criticizing what they are showing us about ourselves that we don't like. It's the opposite of giving a compliment. When we compliment someone, it is most often because we think they have good taste (based on our preferences of course) or have accomplished something we find worthy. The truth is good taste is a very personal perspective. If I like your sweater it is usually because I would love to be wearing your sweater. In this case, the other person is reflecting what I like about myself in a sense. This is more so with an accomplishment. We admire in others what we would like to accomplish for ourselves.

Judging another is the opposite of this. They are showing us what we dislike about ourselves. It is an opportunity to look within, dis-cover where we hold criticism, and work to heal and release whatever that is within ourselves. Those we judge are just a reflection of the shadows within ourselves that are hard to accept. When we view it as an opportunity for growth, it becomes easier to accept. In my own journey, I now welcome this awareness of myself. It means that I am witness to one of my self-judgements which I can then release. It brings a greater sense of my shadow self so that I can accept it, soften it, and move into a place of more self-love. The more I release, the lighter I become, in so many ways.

From Mother Earth

Come before me little child, come before me.
How can you think you have dominion over me?
Just try to imagine your size compared to mine.
You are a small speck upon my vast land,
yet, I respect you.
I give life to you.
I am patient with you as I wait for you to understand.
We are here together.
We are one with each other
and though your presence could be lost
in my vastness
it is not.
Every footstep is marked,
every loving thought received as it nourishes me.
Your presence is great.
Please remember,
Your presence is great.

CHAPTER TWO

From Despair to Discovery

As my year dedicated to healing drew to a close it was ending as dramatically as it began, but for very different reasons. There is no doubt in my mind that when things are falling apart life is truly presenting the opportunity for a positive new beginning. In order to reap the benefits from the new life I was living, I had to learn to trust that life was leading me with love, regardless of how things appeared to my logic mind. Behind the magic and wonder of my new-found friendship with the trees was an underlying current of fear running through my life. It was an old pattern of believing in lack. Along with the joy and wonder that was unfolding for me, was a parallel reality of having to manage my finances and create a stable income for myself. In my determination to believe in love over fear, I was guided, often unaware, into the highest outcome, but it wasn't without effort.

One week before being 'released' from my job I had attended a weekend workshop that was one of those 'buy it now or lose it' kind of deals. The facilitator was an upcoming Tony Robbins type of guy. He had lots of energy and, after his free talk, the audience had the opportunity to attend one of his weekend events at a greatly reduced fictitious price! I bought it. I even asked the woman who sat beside me at the event, who was in line ahead of me to register, if I could travel with her. It was completely out of character for me. I would never be so brazen as to invite myself on a trip that would require several hours of driving - especially with a stranger - and I had my own vehicle. The words were coming out of my mouth before I had time to think about it. It was like I was being pushed by an invisible force in the direction I needed to take.

The weekend was intense. We started Friday evening, going well beyond what I considered to be a reasonable hour to retire. We continued, starting early Saturday morning - learning, processing, and sharing - and we were still going at 11:00 that night! At that point, I was exhausted and completely ticked off that we were expected to be doing silly activities at that hour. Even though I knew that pushing us would make us more vulnerable, which would then open up more potential for change, I was not impressed.

It wasn't until the very end of the workshop, late Sunday afternoon, when it all came together for me. It seems the facilitator really did know what he was doing. Even though it wasn't obvious to me until then, the purpose of the weekend event was to find out what we truly wanted to be doing in life. Undoubtedly, that was why I was so driven to attend. Not only was I unhappy with my job, I now believe the universe was pushing me, knowing that I soon would be jobless and needing a new direction. What I discovered and declared to the workshop group that Sunday afternoon was that, in my heart, I wanted to be developing and delivering workshops. I had taught Reiki years earlier and offered a couple of holistic workshops that received very positive feedback. After the weekend of exploration, that passion surfaced again. Reflecting back, this was clearly another hidden treasure. Turning my focus in a new direction prepared me for what was to come just a few days later when my means of survival came crashing down. As my career slipped away I was holding the seed of that new direction clearly in my mind.

Once I found myself unemployed it didn't take me long to move toward that new path. Every February there is a holistic fair close to where I was living. I enjoyed attending every year to see if there was anything new that I hadn't seen or tried yet. This time, I decided to see what the market was like for my work. I reserved a table and offered mini-channeling sessions, along with some sound healing. It was the first time I had put myself out there like that as a channel and I was attracting a lot of interest. In one of the brief moments I had between sessions, I glanced up and there stood Ernie, a former Reiki student of mine. I hadn't seen him in several years. As we chatted he commented that he had few people he could talk to with the same understanding I had about his interests in healing and metaphysics. He informed me that he had learned a clearing technique called Theta Healing and it had opened him up to a deeper level of work. Much to my delight, he was happy to practice his new skill and, considering what I was going through, I gave him lots of opportunity! Although I didn't realize it at the time, the magic of life was alive in that reunion. I had dedicated my year to healing and healing support arrived.

What better place for a journey of healing to begin than with family. I don't think I was intently focused on healing around family. As a matter of fact, I don't think I even knew there was the need. What I do know is that something shifted in the process of working with Ernie. As fate would have it, Ernie and I had already done some clearing work by the time I found out that I had to move out of the condo. My choice to move to a location that would be closer to family showed me that I was changing in my relationship to them. It wasn't that I intentionally resisted my family before, or had a poor relationship with them. It was more subtle than that. I had always felt separate and different from my sister and mother, and it was reflected in my proximity to them. Now I was ready to be living close by. As I shifted and healed, I saw a warmer relationship with them blossom.

Working with family was just a warm-up for what was to come. Despite my brave and courageous change of attitude and my new expectations for something better, old fears continued to surface as the year unfolded. By the time I moved in June, funds were getting low and there was no one who could back me up financially. I had to figure something out. Even though my logic mind tried to tell me to start looking for a job, I knew that was not the answer. That direction would take me back onto the life course that I had just been kicked out of! Instead, my plan was to apply for a program that offers financial support while starting a business. It would give me the opportunity to start working in the alternative healing field - my true passion - and start developing the workshops that I was excited to offer.

During this time, I was channeling daily with a group of Beings called the Council of Nine. They had asked me to be their scribe during a meditation one day. Similar to my conversations with Henrietta, their messages were collected into my book *The Spiritual Seeker's Guide to Happiness*. My connection with the Council of Nine was also contributing to my healing journey. What I have learned from these unseen sources is that we have actually been socialized not to love ourselves. The Council of Nine once told me we should take the word selfish out of our language. In truth, it is a guilt mechanism to keep us in a state of self-sacrifice versus self love. There were many ways in which that manifested in my world and one was to be living in lack. I began to realize that it stemmed from the limiting belief that I am not deserving of all the goodness the world has to offer. When I learned that we can only love another as much as we are loving ourselves, it made perfect sense to me, and gave me permission to move toward complete self love. I was beginning to understand that self love is not selfish but truly the greatest gift we can offer the world. In contrast, loving from a place of emptiness is not really love at all, it is need. Henrietta expanded on this one day when I asked her what she would like to talk about. I now recognize that her messages were often connected to what I needed to hear. At the time, I thought they were just random insights that she had to share. However, as I reflect back, I see that she was supporting my learning with her conversations. She answered my question by saying she would like to talk about love. "Love?" I questioned, since it seemed to be a recurring theme. She responded by asking, "How could there possibly be too much conversation about love?" Good point! Then I received this teaching about human love:

Love in the human sense is not really love at all but greed. The love that has existed among most — almost all — humans on your planet up until now has been self-serving love. (Not to be confused with self love). You bring someone into your life to meet your needs and call it love. This is not to criticize what has been, for it was a necessary tool for survival. The reason we wish to speak about love this day is because it is time to have a new understanding of what love truly is.

You feel it within yourself Jane when you are connecting to the Earth and your Guides and you are moved to tears — or almost so — by the vibration of what you feel. This is what love truly is. There is no condition connected to it. It is not there to fill a void although it does replace a void. That is to say that, when you are connected to this kind of love, there is no void in your life.

There is no longing or emptiness for the lack of 'another' in your life. There is a beautiful wholeness that wants only to serve. This does not mean that you do not have a Beloved in your life. It means that you do not 'need' a Beloved in your life. When you do have a loving partner in your life, it means that you accomplish so much more together in your service to the Earth and humanity.

We share this so that humans can understand that the old way of being in love will no longer serve their growth and development. It will often keep people from moving forward into their highest potential. For those who know they are in a relationship out of need, we ask you to question that need within yourselves. Are you in a relationship because you are afraid of not being in a relationship? If so, you are not allowing the fullness of true love, which we spoke of earlier, to come into your life. Now, this conversation is not to encourage the ending of relationships. It is to encourage the full potential of who you are as human beings in this time of transition. The greatest love is within the self and for the self. Often, what appears as a loving relationship with another is truly a lack of love for the self. If you are looking for the wholeness of self to come through another then you are lost.

This conversation is to encourage you to find yourself. First you must find yourself in order to then learn to love yourself. This is an important step in the evolution of mankind and so we offer it here as an exploration. We offer it as an opportunity for awareness — awareness of self and awareness of the true meaning of love.

It was clear I needed to move into self-love in order to attract outcomes in my life that would reflect that love, versus my old pattern of attracting based on fear and lack of love. Things were off on the right track as I learned that I was accepted into the first stage of the self-employment program. That news allowed me to stop wondering about my source of income and breathe a sigh of relief — for a while. The challenge was, participants were not allowed to begin practicing their business until the program officially started a few months later. As well, it could be some time before I was approved at the second level by the department that delivered the program. That left me with quickly diminishing funds, and no way of bringing in income, while waiting for the program to start. So, while I was having a wonderful time in my new home with the natural surroundings and my evolving connection with Henrietta and George, there were moments when I felt very insecure financially.

Sometimes the messages from Henrietta would have me yearning for a simpler way of life. I dreamed of a culture where we were living off the land once again and less dependent on the economic system that was such a struggle for me. The struggle stemmed from not having the desire for money while living in a society that requires it. Henrietta once said, *"You are growing and learning how to be in these new times. As you do so, you will be growing out of many of the outmoded models of existence that have been anchoring you into darkness.*" Financial stress certainly felt like darkness for me and I was so ready for it to change. I wondered if our economic system might be one of the 'outmoded models of existence' she referred to. With all of this on my mind, I frequently found myself on the trail lost in thought instead of being in the moment and appreciating the beauty around me. Henrietta was aware of this. Often, she would show me my state of mind and invite me into other possibilities.

Once during this time, I visited Henrietta and didn't feel the same love from her that I usually did. I asked her what was different, thinking it was something about her. Instead she told me to remember to be in the moment and not lose that connection. I took a few minutes to come fully into the present and then connected with her again. Once I was more centered I felt the energy shift into the more familiar connection I have with her. I asked, "If you could tell the people of the world anything, what would it be?" She started by saying, *"I would tell people to be in love – in every moment – in love with what is. Even when what is, is not something humans would normally be in love with."* I could feel what Henrietta was talking about as she shared this with me. It was another one of those moments where I was connected to another reality which makes it hard to describe in human terms. I instantly felt a deep reverence for life – for the mere opportunity to be alive on this Earth. In that moment, I knew that being here on planet Earth is the greatest gift we could ask for regardless of what our reality looked like. It was a moment of understanding that opportunity to be here is so precious that an existence that we would judge as very difficult, such as a beggar on the street, is a great gift of existence. And, as I am writing this, I am realizing that Henrietta was somehow able to lift me out of my human experience, for a brief moment, to touch on an awareness that exists beyond our 'normal' understanding of the very precious opportunity to be here on this Earth. I had the same experience on the park bench connecting with the over-soul of damsel fly. I believe she was trying to move me beyond my worries and lift me into a higher perspective of life. This message speaks to that invitation:

Connecting to nature takes the human mind out of self-criticism and into wonder. This is very good for the soul. When your focus moves away from your internal criticism and into the natural world, you begin to see the wonder in existence itself. By questioning your mere existence on the Earth and your place in the grand scheme of things you begin to take your mind outside of the small, narrow cave that is the thinking mind and you start to illuminate the higher consciousness where the mind can expand and grow. This place of the higher mind is where spiritual experiences come from. It is the place of universal wisdom that the inventors visit to grasp their creations. From this place – which you can connect to by being in nature – all the wisdom and wonder of Divine Mind is revealed. We would invite you as a society to visit there more often. Your North American society is so deeply buried in the intellect it cannot see the simplicity and the purity of life that exists all around it. By stepping out of the small intellectual mind, curiosity would replace criticism – a much healthier perspective for life to be sure.

We are here watching, standing guard for the natural kingdoms on Earth. Most of those kingdoms live in harmony unless interfered with. The human kingdom that has so much brain power is often lacking heart intelligence to create a loving environment for the self or anything in the physical environment surrounding the self. By looking outside of the self and seeing – truly seeing – what exists outside of the mind, humans may find their way back to the heart. There is so much to love in the natural world. Few people can resist a litter of bear cubs in a zoo or a cuddly kitten. Let nature's realm soften your heart and then look inside. You are Creator's child. Creator has nothing but gentle love for you but you must choose it through your life choices. If you feel lost or alone love a tree. We promise you it will love you back – no conditions, no expectations and no rules - just love given freely and with joy. Let the trees show you the way back to your heart. Let the natural kingdom awaken wonder within you once again.

After feeling that deep connection, I asked Henrietta how we can find that reverence in this realm of existence. This is where the teaching expanded:

The beginning is to get out of your mind and into nature – the heart. It is as if nature and your heart are the same energy. It can be a matter of the chicken and the egg. By being in nature you can open your heart and by opening your heart you are more connected to nature. The outcome is a deeper reverence for life. The more you come to revere life, the more you will come to accept that all aspects of life are sacred – even the hardships. The hardships are also beautiful experiences that expand the soul. Sometimes hardships bring you to your knees which was required for you to give up control and allow All That Is to find its way into your heart. You can see in this example how hardship is actually beneficial. So, when you have this understanding, it is the beginning of being deeply in love with just Being.

I understood. The only reason I didn't completely crumble when I lost my job was because I recognized the loss as an answer to my prayers. I also knew that I wouldn't have left on my own, even though I was miserable there. Life had to knock me to my knees and then it was up to me to make the best of that state of vulnerability.

The benefit of not being employed at the job I hated was obvious. However, despite what I was learning from Henrietta, the financial worry was making it hard for me to have such deep reverence for life. Instead I just wanted to go back to my comfortable coping strategy and check out! Even though being in the woods did feel better and I had deep appreciation for my surroundings, when I returned home it was like a reality check and I found myself in a place of unrest and concern. My spiritual beliefs were that being happy, and joyous, and in the moment, would allow the flow of prosperity and abundance to come into my life, but there was always a feeling of disbelief lurking in the background. I was unable to shake a deep fear that I wouldn't get into the program that I was completely dependent on financially!

At the time, I had two ways of managing my fears: being on the dyke or among the trees, and asking Ernie for help. Even though the forest offered some reprieve, I needed to go deeper. I called Ernie. As always, my friend was very generous in his support. I told him what I was feeling and he did some clearing. Then we hit a block. He was trying to help me see that my ego was holding fear around money and I just couldn't see it. I wasn't connecting with it at all. Linking the words ego and money just didn't make sense to me. We were on the phone for almost an hour before I finally was able to get a glimpse of what he was saying and do the clearing. That one was deeply buried!

A few days after my call with Ernie I went to visit Henrietta again. It was fall now and the trail was changing rapidly. As the weather got cooler, the ferns in the undergrowth were dying and turning brown and the leaves on the trees were beginning to change. I made my way to Henrietta and sat on her exposed root as I often did. It was like a little seat at her base. I closed my eyes to connect with her and felt a powerful surge of energy running right up through my root chakra. I was taken by surprise as I had not experienced that before. It seems I may have needed some extra healing energy that day and I was grateful to receive a little unrequested support. The message that followed felt like a reference to what I had gone through with Ernie, working to release my fear and find my way back to trusting life. Here's what she had to say:

Love is the key to all Creation. Creation is Love made to reflect love out into the world – to each other. Love all around. Love cannot heal if people do not let it in. The power of love can conquer all but it takes a willing heart, one that has recognized that love brings life and is the true place of power. Evil has no power over love. If you only knew that you would laugh at the folly that you have lived, letting fear hold you back for so long. This is a reason to love the self. Step into your power of being love and stand strong in the Light of Love like a warrior for Spirit. Strong are they who feel so much love from the Divine that they are invincible. They are invincible not because the physical body cannot be harmed but because the Spirit cannot be harmed. When you realize this, you carry the strength of love and your life changes. Gone are the days of holding fearful thoughts. They are replaced with a knowing of the power that love brings.

Thanks to all the support I was receiving, the foreboding feeling dissipated as I managed to hold the faith that all is well. A couple of weeks later I learned that my application made it through the secondary process of qualifying for the program and my training would soon begin. I was elated! Finally, I could start promoting my business and get to work. I would be moving into what I knew to be my soul's work - offering healing and workshops.

A couple of weeks after learning that good news, I received a phone call from the person who had done my initial interview to ask if I was in the program. I think she was relieved for me as she explained the reason for her call. Several people, who thought they would soon be running their businesses as part of the program, received disappointing news. Apparently, there was a lack of funds for the program and not everyone could be accepted! I knew in that moment what my fear had been about. There was no doubt in my mind that I could easily have been one of those people had I not released my beliefs around lack. Perhaps my foreboding feeling was not just about releasing subconscious fears. I believe I was also tuning into what was a real possibility of being one of the unlucky ones, left hanging without any financial support at the last moment. I was deeply grateful for all the support I had received as the year unfolded. That news truly showed me the power of love over fear, just as Henrietta had explained. What I had not realized before is that our lives are directed based on the point of view we hold toward our circumstances. I was learning that my determination to stay positive, and clear my limiting beliefs, was attracting the support that the universe had been waiting to give me all along. This was a profound realization. So many times in the past I had been told that I just needed to get out of my own way, and all goodness would be delivered, but I had no idea what that meant. I was beginning to understand that when we stop viewing life through our limiting beliefs – by discovering what they are and releasing them – we then have eyes to see the goodness and grace that has been waiting for us all along.

One day, when I was feeling excited about my journey forward and connecting with Henrietta, she offered this message:

This is a day of great magnitude on your Earth. (When she said that I thought that there may be some planetary alignment that she would tell me about or something happening that I was not aware of. Instead it was a simple lesson). *The sun is shining brightly, unhindered by the clouds. The breeze blows through the leaves as they sway and flutter with appreciation. The shadows play upon your paper as the pen glides. This is the poetry of nature – ever changing, ever growing and ever evolving. So, you humans who read these words, bring yourself to us. Allow us to merge with you, even for a moment. Do not come to feel sorry for us. We are at peace. Come to feel that peace. Come to rest in the love we have to offer. It will open your heart so that you may find that peace within yourself.*

It was a perfect reflection of what I was feeling as I imagined my business growing, knowing I had several months of financial support to make that happen.

As my new life unfolded I was discovering more and more how things are aligned - one thing leading to another. It's a saying we've all heard before but I was beginning to see what it really meant. All the work that I had done with Ernie, to clear and release my fears and traumas of the past, was benefitting me in unexpected ways. No doubt the amount of clearing we did was a part of that. We literally cleared at least once a week, all year long, as painful parts of my past continued to surface. As time went on I discovered a new clearing technique called Access Consciousness. There were enough free videos online that I was able to learn the technique and use it successfully. Because Ernie and I had done so much work together, I was now able to feel the shift in my body when something was cleared. I played with Access Consciousness, using it with friends who were having problems, and could immediately feel the release as their concerns slipped away. The results were so successful that it became part of my new workshop that I developed to offer to my new community. A little more than a year after attending the weekend event where I realized that my true desire was to be developing and facilitating workshops, I was on my way.

The first workshop was a great success. It was called Discover Your Light. In a sense, it was sharing with others what I had learned for myself. I taught several tools on unlocking the deeply hidden subconscious beliefs that hold us back in life and then I used my new skills to clear them. My greatest desire was to support others in realizing and clearing their limiting subconscious beliefs, just as Ernie and the trees had supported me. My world was such a transformation from what it had been only one year before. I was my own boss, setting my own hours and doing what I loved to do. Along with the deep appreciation for the way life was unfolding, I continued to release and clear anything that came into my conscious awareness as a fear or life pattern.

As these remarkable discoveries were unfolding, so was my connection to the land. Although I thought I would be living in my little apartment forever I was soon reminded that life is all about change. The day my landlord cut down several trees outside my living room window to reduce the chance of moss growing on the roof, was the day I knew I was moving. It was a small stand of trees but what it offered me was magical. There were young maples, mixed with other hardwood and softwood trees, all tangled up with rambling rose vines that climbed at least fifteen feet up into the branches. One of my fondest memories of being there was one winter day when I looked out onto the snow-covered trees to see a red cardinal feeding off the tiny rose hips on the rambling rose bush. It was so beautiful, with the contrast of the red bird on the white snow, and they are a rare sight in Nova Scotia. I couldn't remember the last time I had seen one. Even more significant, I equated it with love and I knew I was being supported by something greater than me. That something greater is so often delivered to me by nature. Without the trees outside my window, it just wasn't the same.

In my search for a new home I found myself in a nearby community, on a road that I had never been on before, going to check out an apartment. Even though it was winter and everything was covered in snow and ice, I was inspired by the scenery. At one point, the road was just a few feet from the edge of the dyke – a little inlet of sorts, where the water of the Bay of Fundy would reach the dyke at full tide. The shore was covered in huge sheets of ice. Such a scene would often send the chill of winter surging through me but I found myself having a very different reaction. I was moved to tears as I passed that area of the road without knowing why. In my search to explain my reaction, I concluded that the land was talking to me, letting me know that this should be my new home. Even though the apartment was not ideal, I decided to rent it because of my reaction to the land. As I was about to learn, sometimes things are deceiving.

My new apartment was essentially the upstairs of a beautiful, old house built in the late 1800s. The owner was an organic berry farmer which appealed to my love of the land. The property was covered in flowering shrubs, large willows and fruit trees as well as the orchard filled with a variety of berry bushes. There was a large wooden awning joining the barn and the house, covered with wisteria vines that were so old the stems were as large as my arm. I couldn't wait to see them in full bloom! I settled in and adjusted to the fact that I had to go through the house to get to my apartment, and share the kitchen. For years I had been living on my own, so this was different for me, but I was sure this was where I was meant to be.

A few weeks after moving, Ernie and I met at a local pub for lunch and then he followed me in his car to come and see my new home. It was a new road for him as well, so I watched my rear-view mirror to be sure he wasn't too far behind me as I made my way home. Then I noticed he was driving very slowly, barely moving. This started at the same place where I had been moved to tears as the road passed close to the dyke. I had to wait at the stop sign before turning, and let him catch up to be sure he would know which way I went. When he pulled into the driveway behind me I got out of my car and walked back to his to see what was going on. He was sobbing. He told me the moment he got to that same place on the road that I had cried, he burst into tears and could barely see to drive.

The difference between our reactions to the land was that Ernie recognized what the tears were about. He had the clear awareness that there had been a massacre on the land there and it was still holding the energy of the trauma. Immediately I thought of the Expulsion of the Acadians. It was a historical event that happened in the mid-1700s when the British took over Nova Scotia, and neighbouring provinces, and kicked the French off the land. It was the Acadians who had built the miles and miles of dykes that were still protecting the land from flooding as the tides rolled in and out daily. Apparently, the expulsion was more terrifying than my school history curriculum led me to believe. I knew right away that I had misinterpreted what my reaction to the land was really about.

Ernie and I immediately decided to do a clearing for the land. We made our way to the large maple tree on the front lawn and I called upon my Guides to ask for direction. I was told that we should offer sound healing and other things to clear the land and also protect ourselves from what would be released. Then we went back to the dyke and performed the healing. We were given clear evidence that our short, impromptu ceremony had released some of the pain of the past from the land. That experience provided more evidence of the connection between all life on this planet. We are living on this land that is our Earthly mother. We may think we are separate from it, and yet, the fact that Ernie and I both reacted at the same place, in such a visceral manner, speaks to the level of connection that is there. For sensitives such as Ernie and myself, it is as real as what we would consider our daily existence.

After that clearing for the land, another miraculous event happened for me. I soon found myself very discontent with my living arrangement. My landlord was moving back into an old relationship and the house was getting smaller so-to-speak. I wanted out. The only problem, I was only two months into a one-year lease. Again, life showed me the beauty of how things work when we are in alignment with All That Is. Not long after Ernie and I cleared the land, I watched a YouTube video by one of my favourite-at-the-time spiritual teachers. It was no coincidence, I am sure, that it was about releasing unwanted contracts and I immediately thought of my lease. She gave all the details of going into meditation and what to ask for. I followed her advice and asked for all contracts that no longer served my highest good to be nullified, or something like that. What followed was almost unbelievable. The *v e r y   n e x t   d a y* my landlord sheepishly asked if we could meet that evening. He told me that he was giving me three months notice to end the lease because his girlfriend was moving in and he needed the space! I could hardly believe what I was hearing. He also paid me a month's rent to make up for the inconvenience! I was amazed at the swiftness of my request. I was gone in two months with no penalty and a little extra funds to help with my move.

There is no doubt in my mind that I was called to live in that apartment so that Ernie and I could heal the land. Even as I write this, years later, I am deeply moved as I type these words. It is confirming for me the truth of it. My short stay there took me away from Henrietta and George but into an unforgettable experience with the land. It was a clear indication of our abilities as humans and the power of love over fear. No wonder Henrietta spoke so frequently about love. Every bit of work we do to release our fear and pain from the past leads us closer to it. My experiences were certainly proving that. To offer Henrietta's perspective, this message gives great hope for us all in creating a new reality based in love. Just as Ernie and I released fears and trauma from the past, and together we released trauma from the land, we can all play a role in the creation of the future of humanity and the Earth, based on love. Here, Henrietta offers some advice on how we can all participate in creating a new world full of love:

We would like to speak to you today of war. There are nations on your Earth that have been warring for eons of time. They continue to do so in the name of God – Allah. This is creating a disturbance in the atmosphere of Earth from their warring minds, full of hatred. This can be easily balanced out by people who carry loving thoughts. We would invite those who would be of service to the world by emitting love to do so on a daily basis. Simply love everything – your family – your friends – your home – your surroundings – your career. Whatever you give thought to that fills your heart with love will help to balance the energy of war and hatred on the Earth. Love is like a burning fire that wipes out hatred. It is alive and electric whereas hatred is dead and heavy. You have no idea how significant this loving energy is. It gives others the ability to rise into a place of love as well. By putting your grace into the world, you are changing the vibration. The Earth can use your support right now. She is holding the balance but, in this time of transition, where so much is changing, it is much easier for her when there is a more resonant balance of love over hatred and war.

Soon a time will come when war cannot exist on this Earth. As she transcends the third dimension into fifth dimensional reality you will come to witness peace and joy. Those who would be at war will destroy themselves, no longer taking peaceful, innocent citizens with them. This transition phase is when it is vital to be adding your loving vibrations into the world. And know that you are changing the world in this way. You cannot say that there is nothing you can do because you are just one person. It simply is not true. Your love is felt – always. Your love makes a difference,

Be gentle with yourselves. That is where love starts. Forgive yourselves for those days when you forget to be loving or cannot find that space within your heart. You are human in a dense reality. You are doing wonderfully. For those who would choose to read this material we know that your hearts are pure. You are grace upon this Earth. The human experience is one of feeling many emotions and so you fluctuate from day to day. Accept them all as perfect. All experiences are opportunities to learn more about who you are. When viewed from this perspective, the 'bad' days are as valuable as the 'good'; no right or wrong – just experience. This is the way of the Master and you are all becoming Masters. You already are Masters, you just don't know it. You have forgotten. But we see into your hearts and we know who you are and we love you so.

Love is the way out of war. Of course, this is an understatement. It is an obvious truth. The difference in what we are stating is that it does not have to be the ones at war who find love. Just create a balance of more love than hatred on this Earth and war will diminish. It will not be able to find a vibration that will support it. This is the new way of being – each person affecting the whole with conscious awareness. We hope this brings you some understanding of your role in the world. No one is insignificant – no one!

There is so much wisdom in that message. As I turned my focus away from fear I came closer to living in peace. The trees guided me there and opened up possibilities that I never knew existed.

In time, I could no longer keep the tree wisdom to myself. I started to share the great teachings I was receiving with my friends. Some of my friends jumped right in and were happy to test their own abilities in connecting with trees. Others were more skeptical, which I could certainly understand. Knowing that Henrietta asked me to be her scribe so that I would share her messages with the world, and knowing they would be received with varying levels of doubt, I decided to look for research that might support my abilities to communicate with trees. What I discovered was beyond what I would have hoped for. To my delight, science was validating my experiences with the trees.

Teaching Moment

In this chapter I mentioned that I 'closed my eyes to connect with Henrietta' and later that I 'journeyed within' to connect with the damsel fly. If you are wondering how to connect this way, the most important thing to know, in developing this ability, may surprise you because it is simple. What we often dismiss as merely imagination is in fact a powerful connection to another level of existence. As part of my hypnotherapy training I learned that the subconscious mind doesn't know the difference between imagination and reality. That is why athletes can improve their performance by imagining themselves succeeding. Brain research shows that the same areas of the brain light up when imagining doing something as when the body is actually doing it.

To relate this to connecting with a tree or anything else, it is important to know that what may seem like your imagination is actually a vibrational connection, kind of like telepathy. The only way to discover this for yourself is to give it a try. To begin, you will want to center yourself by becoming fully present into the moment and fully present within yourself. Imagine that you are bringing all your awareness inside your body. Intention is a powerful tool because what you intend you create. It is as simple as intending that you are pulling your energy body into your center – into the heart. Come fully present into the moment and fully aware of being in your body.

There is a part of our Being that knows everything that happens around us. This is the subconscious. Our conscious mind can't hold all this information so it delegates it to the subconscious. Just like our autonomic nervous system, that manages our bodily functions without us having to think about it, the subconscious radar is much the same. It is like having spidey-sense that is always reading the energy field and events around us. A healthy aura is approximately 55 feet in diameter. We are tuning into other people's energy all the time, whether we know it or not. The same is true for the environment. We are not aware that it is happening but, when you consciously bring your energy field back into your body, you may be able to feel it.

As you center yourself this way, and consciously pull all your energy into your body, you are also coming into the now moment. From there, it is a matter of letting your imagination take over. If your intention is to connect with a tree, center yourself and then send some of your energy to the tree. You may want to say hello to the tree and imagine that it is saying hello in return. This gets the conversation going, so-to-speak. Whether it is a real connection or not is less important than just allowing something to come into your awareness, so if you have to make it up, that's OK. In truth, what seems like making it up could be much more than that. There have been times when I questioned my connection until I ask something and realize that the answer that comes through is not something I would typically say or know. By playing with it, you become more comfortable with the process. In time your skills will develop and you may feel more and more sensitive to the natural world around you.

Desire is the biggest component. When I first started channeling I wanted it so much that I pushed it away. When there is a desperation to our level of desire, then it can repel what we are trying to achieve. It is desire that gives us the drive to keep trying, yet it needs to be balanced with a bit of playfulness. Just allow whatever comes to you to flow without engaging the logical mind, which will want to poo-poo everything that comes to you. It is our focus on logic that has kept us from this very natural sense to know beyond what we see with our eyes. It has been programmed out of us. However, it is as natural as breathing. Intuition has been ridiculed in our society for so long that we have dismissed it and the power it brings us. Like all animals, the more heightened our sense of intuition, the more empowered we are to respond to our environment in a way that serves our highest good. Developing this sense will expand your world in ways that you may have never imagined. The result is that you will have access to an infinite source of wisdom that you will learn about later in the book.

For readers who may want to know how to call upon their Guides (or angels), it is a process that takes some practice. There are important steps to take to be sure that you are protected and connected with High Beings of Love. For that reason, I would suggest that you start with the steps offered in the chapter on How to Connect with the Trees. If you are looking for more, you can also visit www.rashana.ca and look at the Channeling Course that is offered there. It gives more direction on how to ensure that you are connecting with evolved Beings of Love.

We Are One

*I dance with the eagle as my mind's eye soars
over the land.
I vibrate with the Spirits of the Earth and I
know that we are connected.
I Am the eagle.
I Am the blade of grass
swaying in the breeze.
I Am the water rushing over rocks to meet
again in the great ocean.
I Am the heartbeat of all life as it pulses
ever closer to Creator.
I Am your brethren.
Feel me dance upon your Soul
and recognize that We Are One.*

CHAPTER THREE

What? Plants Can Read my Mind??

 With the arrival of winter, I found myself more house bound and it seemed like a good time to start putting all my wonderful tree conversations into a book. Despite the depth of my familiarity with Henrietta and George, telling a greater audience that I talk to trees created some hesitation within me. I am not someone who needs proof outside of my own awareness. I have always believed anecdotal evidence because I trust that people know what they are experiencing. However, it is easy to understand why others, who are not having the visceral experience that I am with trees, would have trouble accepting what I was saying about our conversations. For a while that awareness created some resistance within me to declare to all the world that I talk to trees! My solution to this dilemma was to seek out scientific evidence to prove that I am not crazy (out of my mind perhaps, but not crazy). Much to my delight and relief, my inquiry led to incredible research about the intuitive nature of plants. As a matter of fact, it was so compelling, I was surprised that it wasn't common, every day knowledge. The more I looked, the more it seemed synchronicity was leading me to the information that would satisfy my quest. I would turn on the radio and hear something that would grab my attention or go online and have the same experience. I was effortlessly led to scientific studies revealing that plants hold many more similarities to the animal kingdom than we have been led to believe.

One day I stumbled upon a video of a 1979 documentary called *The Secret Life of Plants*. A search on YouTube will lead you to it. *The Secret Life of Plants* speaks at length about Cleve Backster and his inspirational research on the hidden attributes of plants. Backster started his career as a polygraph expert with the CIA, and it was through his work with the polygraph that he first realized the remarkable abilities of plants. His discoveries started when he was sitting in his lab one day and decided to water his plant. He had the thought to hook it up to the polygraph to see if it showed a response to being watered. To his surprise, it showed a stressful response to the cold water. He then had the idea that he would burn the plant to see how it would respond to that. What happened next was quite incredible. The polygraph showed a clear stress response the moment he had the thought of burning the plant! He hadn't even gone to get the matches yet. The mere *thought* of harming the plant caused a stress response! This started a keen interest in learning more about the plant kingdom and led him to many years of research on the 'awareness' of plants.

Realizing that plants are capable of picking up on a person's thoughts, Backster started ensuring that his experiments were random, so that his thoughts would not be affecting the plant's responses to events, and influencing the results. In one experiment, he placed a bowl of live shrimp over a pot of boiling water. He had set up the experiment so that the bowl of shrimp, at a randomly selected time determined by his computer, would tip into the boiling water. He then left his office and went for a walk so he would not influence the results. When he returned, the polygraph showed that his plant reacted at the exact moment that the shrimp had been tipped into the boiling water. His plant was responding to the loss of life of the shrimp! Further experiments by Backster showed a stress response in his plant when boiling water was poured down the sink. He assumed the plant responded because there were live bacteria in the drain that were being killed by the hot water. Bear in mind that Cleve Backster was considered an expert in his field with the polygraph, and he worked for the CIA. It's not like he would be misinterpreting the readings or coming from an airy-fairy state of mind.

Bringing forward information that lies out of the greater understanding of society can be challenging. Cleve Backster dedicated his life to research on plants and never gave up trying to enlighten us on their amazing attributes despite much disregard from the rest of the scientific community. It seems humanity wasn't quite ready to be so at one with nature! Perhaps that explains why Matthew Silverstone, author of the book *Blinded by Science,* discovered a variety of peer-reviewed scientific studies that have been all but hidden within our libraries without any recognition for their findings.

In Chapter Seven of *Blinded by Science,* Silverstone introduces another pioneer who discovered the similarities between the plant and animal kingdom - J.C. Bose. Bose was a professor of science back in the late 1800s and early 1900s whose work was greatly dismissed by many in the scientific community. However, Bose's brilliance is evident. Even though he was the first to prove that radio waves could travel through the air and be collected at a different location, the invention of radio waves was credited to someone else two years later. Silverstone speculates that Bose's

Indian ethnicity may have led to that discrimination. Part of Bose's discoveries was that plant tissue and animal tissue show similar electrical response to a stimulus. Bose took this a step further showing that even metals, what most of us would consider inanimate, will show a similar response to that of plants and animals. For example, metal will show fatigue from being over-stimulated and even 'permanent irresponsiveness' which we would call death. According to Silverstone, Bose "determined that plants were behaviorally identical to animals." In fact, Bose showed that plants are actually more sensitive than us humans. They respond to wave lengths much shorter and much longer than we can see or sense, which means that they are even more sensitive than we are.

Jump ahead 50 years after Backster's discoveries with the polygraph and we find a few brave scientists who are willing to step out of the accepted reality about plant 'behaviour' once again. A man who is passionate about plants and their similarities to animals is Stefane Mancuso, Professor of Horticulture and the University of Florence in Italy. He argues that "99.9 percent of a plant's biomass behaves as animals do."[1] An article posted on The Guardian's website quotes Mancuso as saying, "Humans have five basic senses. But scientists have discovered that plants have at least 20 different senses used to monitor complex conditions in their environment." For example, they can "measure humidity, detect gravity and sense electromagnetic fields." If plants can detect electromagnetic fields, that would explain how they sense the presence of humans. Mancuso also informs us that plants must calculate the quantity of resources to use to solve a problem. He says, "… plants don't just react to threats or opportunities, but must decide how far to react." [2]

Evidence of this came to me in a video I once watched about a reserve in Africa that was experiencing the death of many of their deer-like animals (I forget the name) during a drought. The puzzling piece of this was, on this particular reserve, there was a certain tree that was surviving the drought which meant that this herd would have plenty of food to eat as opposed to other areas where most of the vegetation had died. Despite this, they found animal after animal, dead on the ground, without any evidence of predation by another animal. They were in perfect looking condition but dead. They were so puzzled they called in a team of scientists from the nearby university that were, over time, able to figure out the problem. The trees were being over-grazed because there were so many animals feeding off them, and they were the only vegetation available. As a result, the scientists found that the trees started producing so much tannin that the animals grazing off them weren't able to digest the food, and they died. Not only that, the team discovered that the trees that were being over-grazed were sending a chemical signal to the nearby trees that weren't being over-grazed. The result was, all the trees started producing toxic levels of tannins whether they were being over-grazed or not. This is a powerful example of the intelligence that Mancuso refers to. Under normal conditions, the animals could graze the trees without any harmful effects. It was only when the survival of the trees themselves was threatened that they produced such high levels of tannins.

An article on National Geographic's website states that "new botany is suggesting ... that plants are sensitive and problem-solving but bypass the need for self-consciousness and brain activity that we assume is necessary for intelligence." This ties in with what Henrietta has said about being a tree. They accept what is, while holding the energy of love. In a sense, they don't have the self-consciousness that would make something 'right' or 'wrong'. This, however, does not mean they don't have intelligence. The article goes on to say, "People who think that plants show intelligence are often accused of being anthroprocentric, believing that plants are behaving like humans. The philosopher Daniel Dennett marvelously riposted that critics of this theory are "cerebrocentric", believing intelligent behaviour is not possible without the infinitely superior human brain. What the new work shows is that plants, by means we do not yet fully understand, are capable of behaving like intelligent beings. They are capable of storing, and learning from, memories of what happens to them." This defense of plant intelligence is coming from a well-educated man. Dennett holds a BA in Philosophy from Harvard and received his Doctor of Philosophy at the University of Oxford. At the time of this writing, Dennett is the Co-Director of the Centre for Cognitive Studies at Tufts University. His accomplishments include being named 2004 Humanist of the Year by the American Humanist Association.[3]

Further proof of the intelligence of plants comes from Susan Murch, Associate Professor of Chemistry at University of British Columbia – Okanagan. I was delighted that a fellow Canadian is offering ground-breaking work in the acceptance of intelligence in the plant kingdom. Murch is also the Canada research chair in natural products chemistry. She is fascinated by the "chemical connection between plants and human brains" and has made some remarkable discoveries in her work. One study, published in *The Lancet* in 1997, reveals that the herbs feverfew and St. John's wort "produce hormones such as melatonin and serotonin, which humans use to modulate sleep and mood."

Murch found that suppressing those hormones in plants, with drugs that are prescribed to humans such as Prozac, affected the plant's development. The root system, in particular, was irregular. This is fascinating because, it is speculated that the root system is the area of 'intelligence' in a plant.[4]

Murch's work caught the attention of Anthony Trewavas, Senior Plant Scientist at University of Edinburgh. Trewavas describes intelligence as "the ability to sense one's environment, to process and integrate such sensory perceptions, and decide on how to behave." When we think of animal behavior, it is easy to see that the definition applies. If plants respond in the same manner does it mean they are intelligent as well? Monica Gagliano, of the University of Western Australia, may have the answer to that question. She has shown such 'intelligence' in plants with some fascinating research. She decided to use the same methods with plants that are used with animals, to determine the ability to learn. She used the Mimosa plant because it has a reaction to touch that is easy to track. The plant has a series of leaves along each stem that will fold together when touched. That is, when they feel threatened they will pull in their leaves. Gagliano set up an experiment where she dropped the plants several feet onto a piece of foam to soften the landing. The plants initially responded to the fall by curling up their leaves. However, after being dropped only four times, the plants stopped responding, which showed they no longer felt threatened. They had learned that the drop was not harmful so they didn't need to react. To test that the plants weren't simply fatigued, which may have led to the lack of response, a different stimulus was applied, to which the plants showed their usual stress response. The amazing thing is, the plants remembered what they had learned up to 50 days later. Despite her evidence being solid, Gagliano's work was refused publication because she had the words 'plant learning' in her title, which she refused to change. According to Gagliano, that is just what happened. Although it is not accepted by all, science is starting to show that, despite not having a brain, plants do show intelligence.[5]

Going back to Backster, whose studies have shown that plants have the ability to know our thoughts, is it such a stretch to think that we can do the same and know the thoughts of plants? Of course, you know my answer to that. I believe that my ability to receive information from trees is two-fold. First is my inclination to believe that anything is possible. I know that we don't already know everything there is to know. Secondly is the awareness that, as the vibrational level of the Earth increases, the veil of forgetfulness is thinning between the life we are living now and past life experiences. More and more in my business doing clearing work with people, I am seeing past lives having a strong influence on people's current reality. We are unconsciously remembering information from past lives. I believe that explains what is happening for me in my deep-feeling connection to nature. It is a remembering of times when humanity lived more connected to the land. For example, I had a lifetime in Lemuria where I swam in the ocean and communicated with the dolphins. Perhaps it is that lifetime, and others like it, that create an unconscious awareness within me of our ability to connect with the natural world that surrounds us.

In the evolution of our beliefs we have moved from thinking the Earth was flat, to realizing it is round, to thinking that atoms were the smallest unit of matter, to the discovery of quantum physics. We continue to discover the minute world of the invisible, such as quarks and the potential that atoms are black holes! The more we discover, the more we realize we weren't seeing the whole picture. Without being open to the idea of *Henrietta* 'talking' to me of course I never would have made the connection. Instead, I became aware of the incredible and complex natural world that we are a part of. Perhaps soon, experiences such as my visceral connection to the natural world will be well understood as part of unity consciousness, meaning we are connected to all life!

Henrietta spoke of this connection one day in our conversation. She said, *"Long ago, in the times of Lemuria, you were At One with nature. Those were times of peace. For when you are connected to that nature – the nature of being human in full understanding of your Earthly connection – then you have no desire to cause harm to anything or anyone. You are connected to the heart nature of all life. And we say that all life has a heart nature. To think that nature exists in this perfect balance* (when unhindered) *without wisdom is truly foolishness. The times that you are moving back to will embrace more of this understanding."*

It seems, perhaps because of my sensitive nature, that I have a connection to that 'heart nature' of all life. An indication of that came from an experience I had, long before I started talking to trees. It took me completely by surprise. It happened back in the late 1990s. I was offering healing sessions at a health fair when someone opened a book with pictures of water crystals photographed by Dr. Emoto of Japan and said, "Look at this Jane." I immediately burst into tears and had to ask her to close the book because I was with someone at my table! My only explanation is that the image of the water crystals touched on some deep awareness within my soul of a profound recognition of the beauty and sacredness of the natural world.

As I went on to gather evidence that might explain and support my connection to nature I was delighted to receive this information from George. As I approached him one day he connected with me, full of joy and happy to greet me. I then asked him how a tree could have such a personality. His answer is fascinating and represents a level of knowledge and understanding that is far beyond 'the norm' of our reality but resonates as profound truth for me. It also supports Cleve Backster's work and may explain the source of intelligence for all plants. Here is his answer:

Why would a tree not have such personality? It is a part of life, like everything else. Not all intelligence comes from the brain. **Where does it come from?** *It comes from the field.* **How does personality come from the field?** *The personality of a tree does not come from the field. It comes from the ener-genetic make-up of the particles that make up tree. Your science has proven that animals have intelligence beyond what was previously understood. For example, experiments with crows show an intelligence that has surprised the scientists. It seems to surpass the relative size of the brain. So perhaps not all intelligence comes from the brain. There is intelligence in life itself. There is intelligence in a plant and it has no brain. Your experiments have also shown that plants respond to human thought. How can this be without a brain? And so, to take it a step further and state that plant life has personality is really not a big stretch.*

To address the intelligence of a plant to respond to its environment, including the thoughts of humans, is to realize that all life is connected. One thing does not happen without affecting another thing in its environment. Eventually, this ripple effect passes throughout the entire Earth. Can you see here the significance of every thought? As humanity begins to awaken to what is beyond the understanding of the third dimension, more and more will open to this understanding. The personality is an extension of this intelligence. Animals have personalities and plants do as well. A plant's personality is based on the particles that come together to make up that plant and what those particles have been before. Your quantum physics is now showing that all matter comes out of the field. When matter is destroyed, through death, then those particles return to the field to become something else. They carry the resonance of that which they were before and therefore that becomes part of the personality of the new creation – be it a plant, a person or a snake. All life has its own particular character. There is the character of the species and, more minutely, the character of the individual that is part of that species. This is true of plants, animals, birds, rocks, water. When you consider that all of this planet consists of water and the proof that has also been shown in science that water holds intention, then it can be easier to understand how matter holds character or personality. It is all very simple if you don't complicate it.

...You have to discover what you do not know. Those with an open mind and a willingness to listen with a different aspect of their human self are those who discover the unknown. Just as with Einstein and other discoverers, it is the willing mind that is open to receiving what was previously forgotten, that can bring forth these intangible knowings.

With that, George and I exchanged a few more words and then he seemed to withdraw out of the joyful, dancing personality and went back into being tree, still and silent. It was the first time I had experienced the exchange end in that way.

George's reference to intelligence coming from the 'field' was also told to me by Henrietta. I once asked her how she could have such wisdom and intelligence to share with me, being a tree after all. Her answer was that she pulled her knowing from 'the field'. She added that humans have this ability as well, we have just forgotten. She said that those who channel, like I do, access information from the field but simply are not aware of it. A few days later I was on YouTube, watching a presentation by Gregg Braden – filmed in Italy in 2007 – and he said something that fascinated me. He told his audience that he had been invited to a scientist's lab where Einstein's brain was stored. Scientists had kept Einstein's brain thinking that, because of his intelligence, it might look different than most people's brains. It turns out there was no significant difference, but that is an aside.

Braden informed his audience that the scientists in this particular lab were researching the possibility that memory is not stored in the brain at all but instead our memories are retrieved from an external 'field'. They speculated the brain is more like an antenna that would retrieve memories from the quantum field much like tuning into a radio station. It certainly seems to confirm what Henrietta and George shared with me. It also would explain how all things are connected and how I could know the thoughts of trees and they could know our thoughts. We are all swimming in the same great field of information and potential.

This material may shake up our concept of reality, yet science is always leading us to a deeper understanding of what reality truly is. To bring you information about quantum research and all that it is revealing about the hidden aspects of life I turned to another fascinating YouTube video based on the book *The Holographic Universe*. In Part Two of the video it talks about the research of a brain scientist named Dr. Karl Lashley who, in the 1920s, found that "no matter what portion of a rat's brain he removed, he was unable to eradicate its memory of how to perform complex tasks it had learned prior to surgery." This again supports the idea that memory is not stored in the brain. Jump ahead almost 100 years and we find ourselves exploring quantum physics which may be able to make sense of Lashley's discovery. Quantum science likens our life experiences to a hologram. Dr. Karl Pribram, who is a neurosurgeon and neurophysiologist, also studies where memory is stored in the brain. Pribram set out to solve the mystery of Lashley's discovery with rats. In short, Pribram came to believe that memory does not travel through neurons but through "impulses of light that crisscross the entire brain" like a hologram. *The Holographic Universe* video states that Pribram believes "our brains mathematically construct 'hard' reality by relying on input from a frequency domain."[6] Pribram concludes that the brain's role is to receive waves from "a frequency domain" and interpret that information into the physical experience that we call life. It seems science is supporting what Henrietta and George have shared with me.

In my very first visit with George he addressed this, telling me, "*I pull love out of 'the field' of All That Is. It is like the love is floating around the ethers and all I need do is access that and send it to you. It is very easy and more and more humans are waking to the potential of that.*" I was intrigued and asked if he could help us humans know how to do that. He answered, "*You all do it to some degree, you just don't realize it. As you learned Jane, the mind does not store memory, it pulls memories out of 'the field'. Once this becomes known it is much easier to believe that you can access love from the field or deeper wisdom or whatever you want to know. You have access to all history and also to the future. All you need to do is quiet yourself and pretend you are going into your memory to retrieve the information you seek. It is only your doubt that keeps you from being successful in this regard. You have the tools; you just need to* trust *that you know how to use them.*"

Here's another message from George that may help with the understanding. Some of the information he told me is truly mind blowing, and yet it is so simply presented it would almost be easy to overlook its significance.

Trees have an overview of all life. We stand as sentinels of the physical world and yet we also are connected to all life everywhere. We know the birds and the bugs and the wind and the rain. We know it. We don't just endure it – we know it. This is something that humans can be at one with as well, but you are not. You have been lost for so long that you have forgotten. To 'know' these things is to be a part of their essence. I stand as tree and yet I know that I am not tree. I am particles come together to represent tree. And bird is particles come together to represent bird. And wind is … you get it. With this knowing, I do not identify with tree as such, but with *All That Is*. I am not tree, I am *All That Is* presenting as tree. This is confusing for some, for many of you do not have the understanding of how life is created. You are moving into times when many are telling you that life is what you create. This is what we are referring to here. Knowing that you create with your mind will help you understand what I am saying. If you cannot connect with the reality of that awareness, it is hard for you to understand what I speak of.

To grasp what I am saying, allow yourself to imagine that everything in your awareness is an interpretation, which it is. It is a visual that goes through the eyes, is then interpreted by the mind and becomes an understanding from there. It is your awareness, your perspective, that creates your life. One person can experience a movie and come out with a totally different feeling from someone else who just watched the same movie. It triggers different emotions and pulls on different belief systems for each person. In this way, each is creating their own experience.

This is what we would like you to understand. Your experience is made up of your internal systems of thoughts and beliefs. If you believe that life supports you and that mostly good things happen to you, that is what you will create in your experience. What you create out of the particles that quantum physics calls the field, is good experiences. Another person could be standing beside you or driving behind you and believe that life is hardship and nothing goes right and have a totally different experience. This is just another way to say that the human experience comes from thought. The human believes that s/he is separate from all life and does not see that the field is all life. S/he has the experience of being a thing – a human that believes it is separate from the rest of creation – whereas a tree knows that it is not a thing, it is just the particles of all life coming together to appear as a thing. It appears as a thing because a human believes it is such. What the human believes, the mind will create for the human to see. A tree presents as tree but does not solely identify as tree. It identifies as *All That Is* presenting as tree.

Place your hand on a tree and the separation will not be so strong. You will feel the connection. You will feel the tree sharing itself – its particles – with you, if you are open to such a feeling. If you do not believe it is possible then you will not feel it because, again, you are creating your world. We are expanding your mind here. This is our experience as tree. It is why we can emanate so much love into the world. It is why we can be cut down en masse and not have hatred or regret. We are love particles come together to give you the experience of tree and we 'love' to send our energy to you. We see and know that humans need love and so we offer it to you. If you believe that love is your experience then you will say yes to it and receive it. We will be happy then, for we will have fulfilled our intention which is love. The particle field in which all matter comes to life is nothing but love.

This is a very new concept and it astounded me that George would be sharing something so …. advanced. This information was cutting edge research at the time when it was being offered by George - even in the field of quantum physics. Perhaps this is proof in itself of the ability to pull all wisdom from the quantum field. What stood out the most for me was the word *ener-genetic* in reference to particles holding memories of what they were in a former configuration. That is not anything that I had ever heard before so it certainly didn't come from any level of my previous awareness or learning. At the same time, it makes sense to me – similar to memories from past lives influencing one's current incarnation. It also is similar to what Bruce Lipton, Ph.D., shares with his readers in *Biology of Belief*.

Lipton is another scientist who knows rejection because his findings do not fit the accepted reality. His research reveals that the environment that our cells exist in contributes much more to their regulation and response than chemical signals triggered from our body. The environment that he speaks of is electromagnetic in nature, just like our thoughts. Remarkably, Lipton explains in his book that "The speed of electromagnetic energy signals is 186,000 miles per second, while the speed of a diffusible chemical is considerably less than 1 centimeter per second. That is to say, it is not just the chemical reactions in our bodies that influence our cells. Those chemical reactions are incredibly slow in comparison to the response to the energy environment of the cell. As Lipton points out, "the atom has no physical structure" in the quantum world. This validates what George said about 'presenting as tree' as opposed to Being a Tree. It seems that George understands that he is not physical matter, just as Bruce Lipton explains that "atoms are made out of invisible energy, not tangible matter!"

This can be a lot to take in if it is a new concept. And yet, it is very exciting that quantum physics is starting to prove what metaphysics has been holding as truth for centuries. And, it explains how trees can tap into the great wisdom of the field, knowing that our biology is actually much more influenced by that field than the internal workings of the physical body. As I noted, recent studies are also showing that the brain responds to imagination and what we call reality in the same way. Studies reveal the area of the brain that lights up when someone is having an actual experience also light up when the person is imagining the same experience. The same parts of the brain are activated. As a hypnotherapist, I am aware that we can seemingly change reality through the subconscious which many would call the imagination. Someone who has stage fright can be released from that fear through hypnosis by going into the subconscious and changing the experience that created the fear in the first place.

So, what is real, the original experience or the released experience where the person being hypnotized is suddenly over their fear? I also read that people with split personality disorder can have a diagnosed illness when presenting in one personality that does not appear in another personality. So, a person can, from one minute to the next, go from having a physical condition to not having it! If our bodies are solid reality how would this be possible? Is the illness actually manifest in the body, or does it exist in the mind? I believe quantum physics, and the unfolding discoveries of 'the field', as well as the studies on the brain and where our reality actually originates from, provide the answer to that question. Just as the trees said earlier in this book, I believe we are particles held together by love versus the solid reality that we think we are. For me, it brings great excitement to know that we can access all the information we seek or need through our expanded awareness. By believing it is possible we open ourselves up to the opportunity that all can access this wisdom.

The benefits of being more sensitive to one's environment are described in the following message from Henrietta. She is deeply aware of the subtle shifts that we are going through and the potential to expand our reality as a result of it.

There is much I would like to share to guide you into these new times and the new energies of the Earth. The trees know that the shift has happened because we are very in tune with the energetic field of the Earth and all life forms upon the Earth. When the shift happened on December 21, 2012, the less sentient beings of plants and trees and many animal life forms, felt the change. We are in tune with the subtle energies of the Earth, and so that is why animals can know when an earthquake is coming or a tsunami. The trees, connected to this subtle energy, felt the shift on that date. It was subtle. It was not like a huge lightning clap from the sky as you know, but it was there. It was a difference in resonance and therefore in the sound and vibration of the Earth. With that shift, all life forms were and are affected, including man. However, most humans are not in tune to these subtle energies and so did not consciously become aware of the change. Yet, your subtle bodies did recognize a change. If you will pay attention to the underlying feelings that are part of your everyday experience, we believe you will find that life feels just a little bit easier. For those who are aware, it was felt more clearly than for those who do not walk in awareness. If you are living mostly in the mind and not in the fullness of life on Earth, then you could miss it, even though the mind is impacted by it as well.

A shift really did occur. The way in which it affects matter on this Earth is that all life everywhere can exist in a lighter form. Our molecules are less dense than they were before the shift. For this reason, you can see through things more than you could before. This has a double meaning. For, in your english language, to see through something means that you are not fooled by the outer façade. You can see what the truth is. You can also take this more literally. The molecules that make up the objects that you identify in your life, are now farther apart, therefore less dense, and so you literally can see through objects more than you could before. Most of you will not experience this in your lives because you are still holding onto the belief that nothing has changed. It is not in your experience to see through things so you do not. But, as soon as a few of you have this understanding, it will become more and more apparent to you that this is indeed the truth. Your scientists could prove this if they were attuned to do so. Objects that used to have so many molecules per square millimeter will now be less dense. This will work only if they had recorded before this time, the density of life that existed before the shift of December 21, 2012. And so, this realization is part of what also makes life easier in some ways. Life itself is less dense and so your experiences will also become less dense, less heavy, when you allow yourselves to comprehend this truth.

This is simple truth for a tree because we do not have intellect to try to decipher the truth. We live in 'the field' and so have awareness of what is and that is where we derive our understanding. There is no need to decode anything. It is what it is and that is it. That makes life much simpler for a tree and also more .... Divine. To live as we do, without any emotional yearnings or expected outcomes, life is really quite grand. Life is just being. Nothing could ever be wrong because What Is cannot be wrong. (What a powerful statement!) *So, it makes life simple and yet significant. The trees do know their purpose and that is where the contentment comes from. There is no desire outside of being and serving in whatever way a tree can serve.*

Is there more that you would like to know Jane?

Yes, whatever you would like to tell me.

Very good. We would also like to tell you about the life of planets. You see, the planets that surround the Earth are also shifting. All of this solar system is currently shifting. Although December 21, 2012 was the magical date, the shift continues and will do so for quite some time. As the planets shift, the harmony that is the sound of the universe also shifts. Your scientists have discovered that the resonance of the Earth has changed. That is because she ascended into a higher dimension already and so her frequency has changed. This is true for all life. The frequency has changed. If you could hear all life you would know that the tone or sound of all the planets has changed. Since all matter is made of sound, you can see how this will be impacting all life yet in a very subtle manner. That is why some humans are aware and some are not. It depends on the fine tuning of each individual and their sensitive abilities as to how much people feel the change. So, there is a new harmonic tone in your solar system and this is impacting all life. As you resonate at a higher frequency, you move into a higher dimension of being. And so, it is that many on the Earth, as they come into harmony with Gaia, are resonating at this higher frequency.

This is the wonderful thing about these times. All of life is rising into a higher frequency so it makes it very easy for humans to do the same. It now takes great resistance not to move up with the rest of life. Some are willing to hang onto the past enough to create that resistance but it will become more and more difficult as more and more people move up into harmonic resonance with mother Earth. For the trees and the natural world, there is no resistance. The very nature of most animals and the plant kingdom is to be in harmony with the Earth. We follow her ley lines and her magnetic field and her rhythms. Because of this, animals and plants simply flow with what Gaia is doing. Only the human species would resist, thinking that they have a better way. Even you will not be able to resist much longer. Each generation now being born unto the Earth comes in at a higher frequency so the old energies of the Earth will die away and the new harmonic beings will repopulate the Earth. You can see evidence of this with the children that are being born with such knowing and many with what you call psychic abilities. They are simply more connected and, as children, have not put up the mental parameters that would disallow that understanding.

So, we would invite humans to jump in and be part of the new harmonic resonance that is planet Earth. It is really quite beautiful. You have described it, playfully, as a pink haze Jane and we would say to you, that is very close to being the truth.

There is plenty of evidence to prove what Henrietta spoke of regarding people becoming more sensitive and in resonance with the Earth. In the next Chapter, I share some unexpected research that I came upon in my quest to prove that it's possible to communicate with trees. There is an awakening happening, no doubt in response to the higher frequency that we are living in, leading us back to the land. We are returning to our connection to the All.

Teaching Moment

I would like to expand on the reference to Dr. Emoto. For those who are not aware, he was a Japanese Doctor of alternative medicine who invented a way to take pictures of water molecules just before the point of freezing. With this visual description of the state of water, he conducted many experiments, showing that unhealthy water would look like a blob and healthy water would look like a snow flake, with very distinct shapes. He referred to the snowflake-type images as crystals. They form when water is in a purified state. His experiments exposed water to music, words, prayer, etc. with profound results. He showed that praying to polluted water would heal it, the images transforming from a brown blob to a crystalline structure. The polluted water was unstructured and often discoloured. Dr. Emoto's work provided a very visual understanding that water, like plants, is influenced by thought. It also indicated the power of our thoughts to heal, just as prayer and intention restored the water to a pristine state. He has published several books with images of the changes in the water.

I believe my tearful reaction to the vision of the pure water at the health fair that day was a recognition of something beyond our current understanding about water. When I touch on a deep truth, I am often moved to tears, without having a conscious awareness of the depth of what is being remembered. In a message from George he told me that water holds many attributes that we have not yet discovered. For example, he said that we could ask our water to purify our blood before we drink it and it would do that for us. I have also read that water is, in a sense, dead when we drink it from our taps. Beyond the harmful effects of fluoride, the 90 degree angles of pipes is not natural for water. After learning that, I bought a round 4 gallon glass jar to put my filtered water in and I would pick it up and spin it, to create a vortex for the water. I could feel deep appreciation from the water for this movement and would know when it was enough and I would stop. Where I lived in the mountains, I was fortunate to have a natural spring nearby where I got my water, filtered by the mountains! What a blessing. Because of this, I hadn't been spinning my water. However, one day I had some in a drinking bottle and had the thought to spin it and I could immediately feel deep appreciation from the water for the healing movement. There is so much to life that we have yet to discover.

I would also like to expand on George's statement when he said "I Am All That Is presenting as tree." He went on to say it is our perspective that creates our life. I have seen the evidence of this very clearly in my work with the Freedom Release Technique that I created. (www.freedomreleasetechnique.com) It is a clearing modality that allows me to go to the source of someone's suffering and clear it. For example, a person's intimate relationship trouble may be related to a past life they had together. In my work I erase that past life, in a sense, and replace it with something more positive. As a result, the subconscious belief that the client is responding from changes. Intuitively, we often instantly like or dislike someone without knowing why. Often there is a past life connection that is influencing our thoughts about the person, or they are triggering something that we don't like about ourselves. Regardless, the base of the feeling is a hidden belief. When I work with my clients, to identify and release their beliefs, their lives change very quickly. That is also why I was able to change my life so much in 2012. It was the clearing work that Ernie did with me that allowed me to begin releasing beliefs of hardship, lack and limitation. What happens once our beliefs are changed is that our lives change to respond to the new belief, or lack of a limiting belief. I often share the story about believing I wasn't supported in the world. I always felt alone, and created that in my life experience, until I cleared it. I lived alone for 17 years of my adult life. The very day after I cleared that belief, support just starting coming out of nowhere. The immediate shift in my life experience showed me how my thoughts/beliefs create my life experience. When we change our perspective our whole life changes.

Here's another example that I hope will help with the understanding of this. I was once going for a walk with a friend on a nice trail beside a stream. As we were walking along I saw a squirrel and pointed it out to her. Now, it's important to note that this friend is not the nature lover that I am. We live in different worlds that way, you could say. When I pointed out the squirrel, she couldn't see it, even though it was only a few feet from us. I was a bit surprised and said, "It's right there." Still she couldn't see it. So, I pointed it out the third time and finally, after another delay, she saw it. Others may not agree with me, but my explanation of her delay in seeing the squirrel is because she doesn't look for pleasure from nature and take in the environment the way I do. Therefore, the squirrel simply was not part of her experience. I had to give a lot of attention to it for her to bring it into her awareness. To me, this was a clear example of how we create our reality based on what we look for, and what we look for comes from our beliefs.

If you would like to learn more about the impact of our beliefs, you can order my book *You Get What You Believe* at www.rashana.ca or from Amazon. It may help deepen your understanding of this concept. It is a quick read, and yet I have been told that the book has changed people's lives. It's not surprising because understanding the impact of our beliefs on our life experience is profound. What we create in the world changes to match our beliefs. That's why my mantra 'all change leads to something better' led me to a better life. I chose to believe that was true, knowing that what I had been creating from my former beliefs about the world was not worth repeating!

If you have any specific questions regarding this, please submit them at www.conversationswithatree.com.

The Visit

*As the still moon sits in the night sky
I see you come before me,
like mist out of the hollow.
You speak to my soul
in a language I have only to remember.
My very essence resonates with a love
so pure that it must be diluted,
like the moonlight through the clouds.*

I have been touched by the Truth.

CHAPTER FOUR

Feeling Sick? How About a Hike

Can you imagine a world where doctors would prescribe a walk in the forest as a prescription for stress reduction? I hope so, because I'm excited to inform you that it's already happening. The joy of discovering the work of Cleve Backster and others who, I feel, validated my experience with the trees, was magnified by research into the health benefits of the forest. As I was receiving messages from the trees, I had no idea that there were so many studies into the wellness benefits of being in the forest. I was truly surprised to discover that scientists are conducting thorough research into the health benefits of trees and nature. The Japanese have led the way, providing evidence that makes a clear connection between our physical and emotional presence in the forest with improved physical and emotional health. Just like my experience of feeling less stressed once I was in the love bubble of the forest, recent studies are making a strong link between time in nature leading to an overall improvement in health. It seems we are understanding the need to return to our roots.

There's no question our journey away from nature and toward more technology has led to lives filled with stress, illness and a disconnection from our fellow humans. Henrietta described very clearly in the following message, what our lives are like in our hectic, plugged-in world.

You live busy, active lives with very little stillness. This is what brings much of the despair and hardship in your society. It is the lack of stillness. When you think of nature, what do you usually think of? For most people, it is stillness. Of course, everyone knows that nature has two sides, like all things in a duality existence. Nature can be calm and still and it can be outrageous and destructive. That is the balance of existence. We would say that the realm of nature is more stillness than destructiveness. And yet, the human experience is more of a disruptive pattern of living than stillness. Most humans find very little time in their lives for stillness. And so, it is like their lives are similar to a continuous storm. Imagine day after day walking outside into a storm. For months on end, every day you walk outside and it is stormy. In the winter it is snowing and the wind is blowing. In the summer it is rainy and the wind continues to blow. You are always cold and always feel that you must harden yourself to stand against the winds. This is what it is like to be a human in these times. You have created lives that are like living a storm every day. It is the storm of hurriedness and busyness and demands of your careers and travel to and from work. You get home and then the children's activities begin and you gobble down some food and run out the door once again into the storm. This has created much weariness within the human body and psyche.

When was the last time you sat on your doorstep and talked to a neighbour? What, you say? Sit on my doorstep? Talk to a neighbour?? For many of you this would be unheard of. And yet, it would bring you great comfort. It would bring you a sense of belonging – a sense of community. Oh, but your closed hearts will not allow such a thing. This is brought forward to give you an idea of what we are talking about here. The little things that bring the heart pleasure, the slowing down of living, are far from the current reality for so many people on your planet. This is not to say that such people and communities do not exist, because they do. But, there are very few of them in your busy cities. Your city folk have lost touch with the stillness of life. The very thought is repulsive. Many are lost in the hustle bustle because it means that they do not have to look inside. They do not have to stop and wonder who they are. That would be terrifying in itself, and so they continue to run in circles, like a lab rat in a maze, running from the very essence of themselves.

There is much beauty in simplicity. We see that you are slowly finding your way back to that. And when you do, the trees will be here waiting here for you. We will be here noticing. And we will say welcome back. Welcome back to you. For you see dear humans, you are running from yourselves. And the only place where you will find true joy is within yourself. Therefore, you are running away from joy. We are here to help you and guide you. The natural world, in all its intelligence, is here waiting. Walk up to a tree some day and, in your mind, say hello. See how you feel. Do you feel that tree acknowledging you with its loving essence? All of creation is love. Because we do not have the experience of being out of the simplicity of merely being, we have love to share. That is what we are. That is what all of creation is, unless you create otherwise, and even that is love. So, when you acknowledge a tree and offer your love to a tree, you will get it back. If you can slow down long enough to still your heart you will feel it. Try it. It is not for the trees that we ask this. The trees do not need your support. We are full within ourselves. And we have love to share. It is for your experience that this is suggested. It is so that you can experience the fullness of the very world that you live in.

A little 'tough love' from Henrietta was out of the norm for her but I trust it is something we need to hear. Fortunately, we are beginning that journey back into ourselves as the awareness comes forward of what we have lost in our disconnection from nature. I am very excited about this research and welcome the day when others will share similar experiences as mine, and we have a deeper understanding of the many benefits of our connection to the natural realm.

People who live more in harmony with nature already know the benefits of that connection. Studies have shown that the farther we remove ourselves from nature, the less happiness we have in our lives. People living in poverty, in some of the poorest countries of the world, have more happiness than those of us living in the more 'civilized' western world. We have all the stuff and they, living closer to the land with less stuff, have more joy! Why would this be? We have been taught that the more stuff we have – including technology – the happier we will be. However, if you stop and look around, you may find that most people are searching for joy by wishing for things and yearning for more yet never truly satisfied. Perhaps those who live more connected to the land know something we don't - that our stuff is not going to make us happy. It is our connection to nature, to our souls and to each other, where we will find fulfillment. As we return to nature we return to our true essence, just as Henrietta advised.

The health benefits of returning to our nature as animals living on this beautiful planet is validated by research coming out of Japan and Korea. Shinrin-yoku, or forest bathing, was first introduced in Japan in the early 1980s and involves simply spending time in the forest. However, it does require being fully present in the environment – unplugged so to speak. In Japan and Korea medical doctors actually prescribe shinrin-yoku, as a medical treatment! In fact, the benefits of spending time in the forest has become so well accepted in Japan that they have many forest trails officially dedicated to the practice of forest bathing and the government has invested four million dollars in research connected to it! The plan is to have 100 forest bathing trails to encourage people to reap the benefits of getting out of the city and into nature.

As the practice of forest bathing is evolving, studies are showing that as little as 20 minutes in the forest reduces blood pressure and heart rate, increases fighter cells that assist in the prevention of cancer, and reduces adrenaline that leads to stress. As most of us know, stress is the foundation of a long list of illnesses. Remarkably, some research noted that the beneficial effects of a three-day stay in the forest can last for up to 30 days. In these studies, blood and urine samples were taken before and after being in the forest. A control group of people who did not leave the city, were included in the study. Results show forest bathers experience as much as a 40 percent increase in levels of NK (cancer) fighter cells whereas people who walk in a completely urban environment showed no change.

Other forest bathing experiments, conducted by Qing Li, Senior Assistant Professor at Nippon Medical School in Tokyo, and President of the Japanese Society of Forest Medicine, show "that forest bathing trips significantly increased the score of vigor in subjects, and decreased scores for anxiety, depression and anger – leading to the recommendation that habitual forest bathing may help to decrease the risk of psychosocial stress-related diseases."[7]

Li, realizing that most people may not be able to spend three days in the woods, tested participants after a one-day trip to a sub-urban park and found that NK levels were boosted for up to seven days as a result. This research supports what Henrietta encourages - to spend your days off relaxing in the great outdoors.

Forest bathing research supports the work of Richard Louv, author of *Last Child in the Woods* and *The Nature Principle*. Louv discovered that children with ADHD receive the same benefits from 20 minutes in nature as they do from Ritalin! Louv coined the term nature-deficit disorder to describe our disconnection from the Earth. He links it to childhood obesity, depression and attention disorders. In his book, Louv reveals that spending time in nature has other, less physical benefits. The author found that children exposed to green space were more social and more willing to share. Louv's work also shows a beneficial impact for adults, with a distinct change in values after time spent in the forest.

When I first heard the title of Louv's book, *Last Child in the Woods,* I was intrigued. It made me think of my own childhood experiences in the woods and how much it meant to me. I remember being four or five years old and seeing a deer for the first time. It was magical. We were having a picnic with my grandparents, which was a regular Sunday activity in the summertime. In today's world, the thought of going on a picnic seems like a complete waste of time. In contrast, in my childhood, picnics meant getting outdoors, being in fresh air (which was valued back then as beneficial to our health) and spending valuable family time that was free of distraction, other than the sounds of birds chirping and the hope of a rare glimpse of the graceful creatures of the forest.

I remember another time, well into my 20s, when I first hiked to Cape Split, which is a trail on top of Cape Blomidon in Nova Scotia. My friend and I hiked for two hours, through the trees and by a stream, before finally coming out to the clearing at the end of the bluff that towers into the Bay. As we emerged out of the trees and looked out onto the small clearing on the edge of the cliff, there stood a single deer, with not another person in sight. I still remember how special that moment felt to me. To walk out of the forest into the clearing, overlooking the vast Bay of Fundy, and also be blessed to witness the innocence and beauty of nature's graceful inhabitant felt like a gift from Mother Nature herself.

As I moved into my teenage years, the woods were my salvation. They were my only solace from a very troubled home environment. I would let the small, babbling brook carry my tears away with the love tones that sang to me and the trees comforted me with their presence. Later, once I was 18 and finished high school, I was more than ready to leave the nest. My sister and I, along with a couple of friends, hopped on a train with the intention of heading across the country to great new adventures out west. We made it as far as the city of Toronto and ran out of funds. In truth, it was more of an escape versus a carefully planned trip. So, there we stayed – far from the call of the forest and the beauty of nature. After a year of living in the concrete world of that large city, I found myself depressed and despondent. I have often looked back with deep gratitude that somewhere within me I knew I had to return home to the wildness of Nova Scotia. Without it I may have been forever lost. My soul was dying in the absence of nature.

From my experiences of receiving solace from the most challenging times of my life through the support of the forest and being in nature, I can easily accept that a deficit of nature would lead to a negative impact on one's health. What's exciting is how easy it is to correct that deficit. As I mentioned, studies are surfacing to reveal that children, including those with ADHD, who are exposed to green spaces such as parks and wooded areas, are calmer, more congenial, healthier and perform better academically. *Last Child in the Woods* states that natural surroundings support every aspect of children's development – physical, emotional, spiritual and mental.

To accentuate the need for our return to our roots in nature as an alternative to stress management in children (and adults), consider Louv's reference to a study published in 2003 in the journal *Psychiatric Services*. It revealed the shocking statistic that the number of anti-depressants prescribed to children almost doubled in five years and the largest increase (66%) was among preschool children!! He states there is evidence to suggest that the increased need for medication is related to the decreased contact with a natural environment. As the number of studies increase, there is clear evidence that children who live in a more natural environment are better able to cope with the stressors of life. For example, children from rural homes in "grades three through five… with more nature near their homes received lower ratings than peers with less nature near their homes on measures of behavioral conduct disorders, anxiety, and depression. Children with more nature near their homes also rated themselves higher than their corresponding peers on a global measure of self-worth." 8

Indeed, Louv discovered in his research that adults as well feel more themselves – more authentic – when surrounded by a natural environment. I can understand why the ratings for self-worth would be higher for children living closer to nature. When I am in nature it seems to me that my sense of purpose shifts out of who I am in the world, and what I can accomplish – almost as if I have to prove that I am worthy of being here –into simply Being. When among the trees I have a greater sense of being at one with the Divine – attuned to the environment with a sense that nothing more is required.

Many of my conversations with Henrietta brought through information about the need for us to connect with the Earth and nature more fully. She spoke of aboriginal cultures living lives that are whole and harmonious because of their connection to the land. The opposite of that is our modern lifestyle where we are out of balance as we become more connected to our technology than we are with the Earth or each other. Here is what she suggests:

Give yourselves permission to spend time doing nothing. That 'nothing' is really something when it is spending time in nature. Sitting by a stream on a summer's day is not a waste of time. It is the wisest use of time, for it stills the soul as it nourishes the heart. It connects you to your Earthly mother. When you are in resonance with her, you are in good health — you are joyful and feel complete. This is what a summer's day by a stream can do for you. Get out into nature once again and find wholeness in your life. And take your children out of so many indoor activities and put them in nature. Take them to the woods and go exploring. Their growing minds will marvel in all that they see. They will touch the moss and feel its softness under their feet. They will smell the pine needles on the forest floor and inhale deeply. They will find twigs to use as swords of light as their imaginations have time to expand into wonder and they become super heroes. This is much better for a child than another class that is indoors after being indoors in school all day. What better school is there than to expand the imagination? After all, you create with your imaginations. The more vivid the imagination is the more you can create. Take the children outdoors and give them the opportunity to step into the creative mind and out of the logic, structured state of being. Take them away from the smallness of their technological toys and expand them into the vastness of nature. Allow them to grow into their true nature through nature. You will be giving them a great gift. Be conscious of doing this for yourselves and your children, fully present in your mind as you step onto the grass and feel its coolness under your feet. Go ahead, be brave and walk in your bare feet. That is why you have skin, so you can touch things without harming the internal workings of the body. This invitation is given with a deep yearning for humans to find their way back to the wholeness of who they are. You are of the natural world – of the Earth. Remember who you are.

Another time Henrietta expanded on this saying, *What is natural has a divine essence because it came from Divine Mind you could say. This is why, when you connect with the natural world, it is a different connection. It takes you, if you will pause for a moment and truly BE with it, it takes you to a different place within your Being. It takes you out of your mind and into your heart. When you connect with something in nature, you feel good. It lifts your spirits. If you put your children in front of the TV for two hours they get cranky and start arguing with each other. This is not just sibling rivalry. This is spiritual deprivation. Their spirits need sunshine and fresh air. This is so lost in your current society.*

There is love here waiting for you. We embrace you with our essence. Can you feel it? Ask your children if they can feel it in nature? But please do not ridicule them when they share what it means to them to connect to nature. Perhaps they know something you have forgotten. We, the forest send love to you – Creator love. It is what we are and it oozes out of us like sap from the bark, ready for you to notice and here to serve your highest good, for we know why we are here.

If you're a parent, there are more reasons than Henrietta suggests to get your children outdoors. For the first time in generations, it is predicted that my children will not be as long lived as I am. In other words, medical technology is no longer enough to increase longevity. We have strayed as far from our connection to the Earth as we can without destroying this planet and ourselves in the process. Fortunately, the pendulum is swinging back as we realize that our source of life is the Earth and being more connected to her will restore our health and sense of well-being. Evidence of this is everywhere.

One day, as information was coming to me about the benefits of nature on our health, I awoke to my radio alarm and found myself listening to an interview about a new preschool in a neighbouring province where the children spend all their time outdoors. The preschool was based on Swedish studies that showed that children who attended nature preschools performed better in all activities once they entered school than their 'indoor' peers. Children attending outdoor preschools also gain good risk assessment skills, and are less prone to accidents. It has also been found to improve the immune system of the children and the adults who are supervising them. This is in addition to the benefits found in Richard Louv's books. Fortunately for our children and society as a whole, forest preschools are popping up around the globe.

Of course, it's not only children who stand to benefit from more time in nature. Another trend called 'earthing' links good health to literally connecting our feet to the land. It offers more detail than Henrietta suggested on the benefits of walking in your bare feet to make a physical connection to the soil. When I first heard the word 'earthing' I was a bit incredulous about giving a 'term' to something so … natural. In my childhood, we just knew that when summer came we couldn't wait to walk in our bare feet and feel that connection with the land. The term 'Earthing' made it clear to me how far removed we are from that simple concept. Despite my resistance to the word Earthing, I looked into it. I learned that, the reason Earthing is healthy for us is that our bodies benefit from the negative electrons that the Earth emits. Because our shoes are all synthetic or rubber, we no longer get the frequency exchange between the Earth and our feet when we are outdoors, leaving us deprived of the benefit of these negatively charged electrons. Earthing allows us to balance the positively-charged electrons in our bodies, which lead to free radicals, with the negatively-charged electrons from the Earth's surface. Free radicals are linked to inflammation and illnesses such as arthritis and cellular destruction. The negative electrons that are emitted from the Earth seek out and neutralize the free radicals, reducing inflammation and restoring our cells. It appears aging adults in particular, find relief from their symptoms by Earthing. The more we connect to the Earth, the less inflammation we have and the better we feel. After my initial resistance, I decided to buy an Earthing Mat so that I can be grounded even in the winter when I am not spending as much time outdoors. The mat is connected to the grounding wire in your electrical outlet (not the electrical current). When bare skin is placed on the mat, the benefits of the Earth's 'field' are received through the conducting components of the mat. Testimonials reveal that many feel the benefits of the Earthing products for conditions such as arthritis, injury recovery and more. Personally, I was surprised at the results I received the first time I used it. I placed the mat at the foot of my bed so my legs would be on it as I slept. At the time, I had just received some body work that led to releasing in the physical through what seemed like a cold. That night I went to bed so stuffed up that I couldn't possibly breathe through my nose. I had been blowing my nose all day. Much to my surprise, I awoke the next morning, after a great night's sleep, breathing with my mouth closed. I'm quite sure the Earthing Mat grounded my energy and allowed my body to release what may have taken much longer without that support.

There is an ever-expanding flow of research about the benefits of a natural environment coming in from around the world. Finnish studies show that being in nature during your breaks in the workplace reduce sick days and increase productivity. There is a new green trend in office structure that includes more natural lighting and live plants. Research shows that workers feel less stress in such environments, which leads to less costs for the company paying for sick days. In Scotland, hospitals are being developed with more green space because they have found that patients recover faster when surrounded by plants. Patients exposed to plants also leave the hospital sooner and rate their experience as more positive than hospitals without greenery. Even having a pleasant view out the window has beneficial effects for hospital patients. We are re-learning what we once knew, that we are nourished by nature.

As we find our way back to our roots and recognize the benefits of a natural environment, green living trends are finding their way into the construction of our homes as well as offices. Leadership in Energy and Environmental Design (LEED) is a rating system that is considered to be the international mark of excellence for green building in 150 countries. "Leaders across the globe have made LEED the most widely used green building rating system in the world with 1.85 million square feet of construction space certifying every day", according to their website. That's exciting news. This movement is more than helping the planet. As we care for the Earth, our health and longevity will also benefit. Thanks to LEED, architects are seeking certification with new and innovative, nature based designs. Just today, as I am writing this, a story landed in my inbox from Houzz.com, featuring an incredible residential building in Milan that was just completed in 2014. (I love the synchronocity of the timing.) It is a LEED Gold-certified project called Bosco Verticale which means vertical forest. Picture a residential sky scraper, covered with balconies, all planted with trees and shrubs. The entire structure includes 780 full size trees and 17,000 plantings in total, all on balconies.

Fortunately, good news travels fast. The Bosco Verticale has inspired the Tower of Cedars in Switzerland. What the architects may not realize is the effects of such plantings may offer health benefits far beyond the pleasing aesthetics of such an environment. Remember Qing Li of the Nippon Medical School in Japan? He suspected that part of the benefit of forest bathing may be related to phytoncides, which are the aromatic substances, given off by evergreen trees and others, that create the pleasant woodsy scent. Anyone who uses essential oils will understand this as aroma therapy. What his research revealed was remarkable. Phytoncides are produced by trees to ward off pests and, in large quantities, can be harmful. However, at low levels, delivered as aroma therapy, they offer many benefits. Li found that "NK cells in a petri-dish ... increased in the presence of aromatic cypress molecules. So did anti-cancer proteins ... which act by causing tumor cells to self-destruct." Scientists in Japan have found up to 100 of these phytoncides in the forest "and virtually none in city air that's not directly above a park." Remarkably, one whiff of tree essential oil has been shown to be more effective than pharmaceuticals in reducing blood pressure! One inhale caused a twelve-point decrease in the blood pressure of the author of the article where I gained this information, who was interviewing Professor Li. Knowing this, living in a Tower of Cedars may well contribute to health benefits that go far beyond what we currently understand.[9]

There are many studies coming forward that speak of our connection to nature bringing us back to health. For me, the deepest and most profound benefit is our connection back to our true nature as humans. I believe our spiritual self is connected to the natural world. When I am in nature I feel more myself and study participants have said the same thing. Yet most of humanity is lost in a world of technology and man-made structures. These creations have led us away from our nature as beings of love and joy. The more technology develops without a connection to the Divine within us, the more miserable and disconnected we become.

I believe that it is our disconnect from nature that has us so sick and unhappy. I also believe it is that disconnection that has allowed us to take from the Earth without ever thinking of giving back, or maintaining the incredibly complicated and intelligent ecosystems of the natural world. There is a grand intelligence at work in nature. Just look at a flower and consider that it started as a seed and grew into a plant and bloomed and gave off a pleasing aroma. What is it that allowed all that to happen? Oh yes, we know that the seed lies dormant and then rain and sunshine coax it to life. But, what is the potential there that knows what is to happen with the moist rain and warm sunshine? It is the same intelligence that created us humans. It is the same intelligence that allows us to breathe and have thoughts. I call that intelligence soul or love. It is in you. It is in me. And, it is the source of all life. That is why it is vital that we find our way back. The farther we move away from nature the sicker we become. As we disconnect from the Earth and the intelligence of it, we disconnect ourselves from the source of all life.

In her wisdom, Henrietta offers insight into our journey back to nature and what that may mean for us in the following message:

I would like to say to humanity this day that there is great hope now, in the universe, for you to succeed in this great transition into the Light. You have moved more fully into what it is to be human. You will begin to see more and more care and concern for the environment and less tolerance for that which is harmful to the environment. You are moving back to the awareness that all life is connected. Just like the roots of a tree reach out and connect with the tree beside it, your energy fingers – your auric fields – reach out to touch each other. You are always connecting energetically with those around you. Even those living in apartments next to you that you may have never met in person, you are connected to. When you begin to understand this more you will change the way you live. It will begin with your connection to nature and a deep respect for all that is. This includes the creatures of the Earth, the water, your fellow humans, plants and all life. Once you begin to understand the deep connection that you have to all, you will want to take better care of the all.

We, the trees, see this happening now. We see it in the circle of time. It has already expanded to this awareness and humans are already appreciating all life and loving all. It is mending the hearts that have been in pain for so long. As you find your way back to nature, you are softening. As you care for all life you are caring deeply for yourselves. This is the beauty of what is happening now. The more you love all life the more you love yourself, and vice versa. This is so beautiful. We can feel it. That is to say, we can understand the feelings that are unfolding in humans. It is like coming out of a cave that you have lived in all your life and walking into the sunlight for the first time. It is so joyous and warm and comforting. We see humans living simply, with great appreciation for each other and hearts full of nothing but love and the desire to share that love. It is like, in your progress, you are moving back to a simpler life. And every element of life is adored. You are the water and the wind and the fire. Not like they are false gods but that you understand that they are part of your creation and that they have their own true nature.

The stillness that Henrietta refers to, slowing down long enough to still our heart, is scientifically proven to be beneficial to our health. Research dating back to the 1930s has shown that high cortisol levels over a period of time will lead to illnesses such as high blood pressure, depression and heart disease. And what creates high cortisol levels? It is constantly walking out into the storm, day after day. The reverse happens when we are relaxed. The fight-or-flight responses of the sympathetic nervous system can relax. This allows the more restful experience of the parasympathetic nervous system to come forward and bring us into balance.

Henrietta shared many messages about a variety of benefits of being more connected to the land. I find myself yearning for the kind of fulfillment she talks about in this message:

In the time when people lived off the land there was great struggle. Crops often failed and storms blew off roof tops. And yet, there was a much greater sense of satisfaction with life. People worked hard, working the land, growing crops and preparing for winter. Even though it was hard work, it was rewarding work. At the end of the day they could step back and look at something tangible that they had accomplished. They could see the garden growing and the preserves filling the cupboard. All these things contributed to the fullness of their day. And so, at day's end when they were tired, they knew they had accomplished something useful. And they felt the great satisfaction of working on the land, in harmony with nature.

Today you do not have those tangible rewards for your work. What do most of you see as a reward for a hard day's work? It is a silly piece of paper called money. And what does that piece of paper represent? For many it represents pain and hardship and lack. That is what you use as the symbol of your day's work. Can you see how this would leave you feeling empty? There is not the same sense of accomplishment for many, many people on this planet. We understand that some of you are living by doing what you love to do, but for most that is not the case. So, at the end of the day, there is no sense of satisfaction from your work. And then, most of you live in cities. There is no connection with the land. Many people go day after day without ever walking on soil. You walk on concrete everywhere, never touching the living grass or noticing the trees or seeing the flowers. It is that disconnect from nature that has so many feeling empty and desperate.

We are here inviting you to come back to your senses. Use your senses, not just your mind. Nature is very playful if you connect. You can feel the breeze as you walk from the bus to your work place. You can imagine that it is dancing with you, like a romantic lover. You can notice where a little weed is growing through a crack in the sidewalk and have proof of the tenacity of nature. You can feel the sun warming your back and know that it is providing life to you and appreciate that it is there. You can expand your world in this way and get out of the little box that is the mind. There is magic everywhere. Look for it and you will find it. Find it and your life will change. Slowly, day by day, you will change. You will feel more fullness from life. Take your children to the park, not the mall. Do not fill your idle time with more stuff. See if you can find the biggest tree in your community. What a fun activity for children. How many trees can you name? All the trees that are in your neighbourhood (hoping there are some) are waiting to be noticed by you so that they can offer their love to you. It seems like a fickle thought to many and yet, to those who know and who feel the love that is being in nature, it is not fickle, it is profound. You cannot see what you will not look at. You cannot feel love if you will not open your heart. And so it is with the trees, you cannot feel our love if you do not believe it is possible. For those who know it is possible, they are richer for it. They are fulfilled in a way that material goods will never equal.

Your life doesn't need more stuff; it needs more love. No matter who you are, you can find love in nature. Nature does not say you are not good looking enough or tall enough or thin enough or that you do not have the right job to be hugging a tree. Those are not the qualities that we see. We see your light. We see your love light. If it is dim we do our best to illuminate it for you. If it is bright, we dance with you. All of life is from the same source, and that source is love. If you are feeling lonely or frightened or sad, come visit us. Put yourself in nature and cry and let it out and know that we are hugging you with our love. We have no judgement for your fears – only compassion. Come visit. You are always welcome. And we will always love you, no matter what you do. That is what we are. Life just is. You would be surprised at how fulfilling that is. It comes from the very core of creation which is love. How does it get any better than that? Stop searching in your malls for love. Come outside to play. That's where the fun is.

There is an incredible amount of research currently available on the health benefits of being more connected to the trees and all of nature. Perhaps, in our journey back to our roots in nature, we will find what the happiest people in the world know, and what Henrietta wants us to be aware of - nature is good for the body, the mind and the soul!

Teaching Moment

I would like to expand on something I mentioned in this chapter. I stated that children and adults who participate in outdoor preschools have the benefit of an improved immune system. One reason for this could be that soil actually has beneficial compounds that improve our health. It's a bit ironic that we live in a society that is so concerned with sterility and killing bacteria with our cleaning products, when dirt is actually good for us. My ears perked up one day when I happened to hear that soil is a source of beneficial bacteria. According to www.healinglandscapes.org, that bacteria is called mycobacterium vaccae and it has so many benefits you may find yourself wanting to eat dirt! Not only can it make us smarter by improving cognitive function, it may be used to treat cancer and other diseases. Add to that the fact that it triggers the release of serotonin, the happy hormone, and you can see why people love gardening. The bacteria is so effective that it is being considered for use as an anti-depressant. Time to get outside and make some mud pies![10]

Blessed Be

*Blessed be the eyes that behold beauty
in each cloud ~
each pebble on the beach.*

*Blessed be the ears that hear the wind
whispering in the leaves
and listen for the song.*

*Blessed be the heart that rejoices
at each glimpse
of the new dawn.*

*Blessed be your tears
as you touch the Soul of Mother Earth
and feel not her pain, but her Love.*

Blessed be.

CHAPTER FIVE

Our Teachers the Trees

As my relationship with the trees expanded I was excited to start sharing my experiences with others. I was curious to see what their thoughts would be and I was blessed to know just where to start. When I made the move from the city to my new small-town home, I was fortunate to have a friend living close by who invited me to join a small weekly meditation group she was a part of. I knew this group of women would be open to hearing about my conversations with a tree. Living in rural Nova Scotia, they also felt a deep connection to nature, and they were happy to discover their own connection to the trees based on my experiences. A few times, when we were meeting, we would go out into the yard and each of us would place our hands on the same tree and tune in to see what the tree had to share with us. With all of us connecting to the same tree we could compare notes. As we did, my awareness of the trees expanded even more. I discovered that others in the group would get the same 'sense' of the tree as I did. For example, one tree in the yard was indeed a young tree, in relative terms, and it held the sense of being adolescent. It didn't hold the same sense of 'maturity' that other trees did or have any sense of duty about it. My friends who were sensitive to the trees had the same feeling. We also played with hearing the tone of the tree. This came from my awareness that everything holds a vibration and vibration creates sound. I also use sound in my healing practice, so it was natural for me to bring it into our tree experience. I would do my best to duplicate what I was hearing as the tree's tone, and most often it would match what another person in the group was sensing as well.

In the corner of the yard stood another older tree that I felt was the guardian for the property. Again, others received the same feeling as I did regarding the tree holding a sense of purpose. This was the first time that I recognized that trees have a role to play in their environment, similar to us humans having a sense of purpose. I knew that Henrietta was a matriarch of the forest grove she was in, but never thought of other 'roles' that different trees might hold. When I checked in with Henrietta she said trees often held a sense of purpose. She gave the example of a tree in a park that is particularly beautiful, displaying a grand array of blossoms or leaves. Such trees have the role of bringing pleasure to all who enter the park and do so by attracting people into the area in which it was planted. Of course, trees in a park often have the perfect environment to grow in, being well attended and free of encumbrances from other trees. And yet, I sensed from Henrietta that they would take that opportunity as part of their purpose in being. George also offered the same understanding in this message:

You live in a magnificent world along with all that is on this Earth. You humans often feel a bit lost, trying to make life what you would like it to be, and so I would like to address this with you today. You see, as trees, we have no choices to make. We stand and grow and reach for the water with our roots and reach for the sunlight with our branches. We welcome birds and insects onto our branches and we watch the world go by, so to speak. We do not run or play. We just grow. And yet, if you touch the branches or the trunk of a small tree you will still feel the energy of youthfulness. You might wonder how that can be. A tree is a tree. And yet we say to you that trees not only have different 'personalities', they also have different ages and stages just like humans. You see, along with the years of standing and growing comes a certain maturity. After being in a place for a certain number of years, a tree comes to learn what its role is in that place. It comes to understand what its purpose is and what it can offer to the living creatures that surround it. So, a tree in your yard will come to watch over you and project a loving energy toward you and perhaps a protective energy. A tree in a park may feel that its role is to be more showy so that people will admire the park and feel that it is worth having in their community. Trees take on their roles relative to the area in which they are located.

Have you ever known a stand of trees to die all within a matter of years? This is not a common occurrence for trees yet it does happen. The author of these words visited the home where she grew up as a teen and all the stately maples that had surrounded the front yard had died. She knew immediately that the trees did not receive the same appreciation and nurturing that her family had given them and they died, and she was right. As trees adjust to their environment, if that environment dramatically changes, the trees can lose their sense of purpose and die. This is just another reason to love the trees in your area. Let them know that you see them and appreciate them. They will feel more important in their Earth mission when you do.

I was fascinated to learn from George that my hunch about all the maples dying was true. My parents would spend every evening in the summer sitting out in the front yard. The original home owners had planted maples all along the circular driveway. There were probably four or five large maples planted on each side of the front of the house, edging the driveway. One in particular received the greatest attention from my family. It was closest to the house and we often sat nestled under its canopy on hot summer days and evenings, enjoying the outdoors and the sweet, short season of summer. I remember my step-father once saying, "If trees could talk, imagine the stories this one would tell." With that memory, I find myself indeed wondering what that tree would have to share now that I am able to communicate with trees. Sadly, that will not happen, as all the maples that blessed our front yard have made their way back to the Earth from which they arose.

Not too long after I left home my parents sold the house. It was definitely in need of repair and yet, my mother would lovingly care for the property, planting flowers and gardens and doing what she could to create beauty around us. The new home owners let the house go even more and eventually put a mobile home on the property. Many years passed before my curiosity took me back to see the property. At that point, I had young children of my own, and wanted to show them where I grew up. I was deeply saddened to see the stately, magnificent maples that once stood so proudly around the property were either dead or dying. It seemed odd to me that all the trees would die at the same time. My guess is that they would have been 100 to 150 years old at that time. That would match the timeline of when the house had been built. However, sugar maples can live to be 300 to 400 years old, so for them all to be dying at that time was odd. There was no evidence that the dead trees were part of some disease. The acreage that came with the house was full of sugar maple trees that appeared to be thriving. It certainly seemed to confirm what George said about the trees losing their sense of purpose. My rationale for their death was that they were no longer appreciated and loved. For us, they were like part of the family. Of course, this is all speculation but it is a curious phenomenon that they all died at once.

My experiences with my friends, tuning into trees the same way I did, gave me courage to tell more people about my conversations with the trees. I developed a workshop to share what I was learning from the trees and encourage others to develop their own connection. What I found to be the most valuable outcome of these workshops was that others were given permission, in a sense, to share the relationship they have always had with the trees. Of course, anyone choosing to attend such a workshop is going to have a nature connection to start with. And yet, many were hesitant to share their deep love of nature or the deeper connection they have had with trees outside of the workshop environment. Some were talking about their love of the trees for the first time ever. The fear of ridicule, or the thought not being understood, held them back from being open about their relationship with the trees. One of the many benefits that others gained from the workshop was the validation of knowing that they weren't the only one with such an affinity toward trees. The workshop provided a safe space to be able to share and be open about their love of nature and their 'special' connection to the trees. For me, it was a delight to learn that others were having similar visceral experiences with the trees as I was.

At one of my workshops a woman enjoyed the day so much that she invited me to be the entertainment at her upcoming 50th birthday party. She lived in a beautiful home, surrounded by trees, so we were able to go through the workshop without leaving her property. As the day was coming to a close I decided to offer a personal message from one particular tree to each person who was there. They could either ask a question or simply receive a message. Some were given health advice, some were given a sense of their life purpose and others were given solutions to a particular problem. As the messages came through, I could sense how the tree was accessing the unique characteristics of each person, delivering information that was accessed from a 'Higher Source' - the All That Is - as I learned from Henrietta and George. The trees are a vast source of wisdom and knowledge and we can access that wisdom using the information and methods that I offer in the next chapter.

Henrietta also informed me that the trees benefit from our presence in the forest as well. Like so much of the natural world, there seems to be a symbiotic relationship between humans and the trees. Here is what she says about this:

We, the trees, have deep love for humans. For you see, you have the capacity to carry much Love Light in your hearts, so that, when you pass us by, we can benefit from that Light. We can feel it and absorb it into our molecules and use it for sustenance. Just as your hearts have an energy field that sustains you, it can also offer benefit to those whom you encounter. Some humans do not 'see' the trees as they pass by and their Light is more closed down, with their focus in their minds. Others have wide open hearts, mothers in particular, and offer much love as they pass by. This is one way in which trees enjoy humans. It allows us to grow healthy and strong. And we would say that when you connect with us it also sustains you. We offer our love back to you when you are willing to receive. Those who take the time to stop and connect with us get a shot of love as they do so. This is how trees can comfort. We are happy to advise you that the more you connect to nature the more you are supported by it. If you were to put more faith into the knowing that nature provides everything you need, you would soon do everything you could do to protect every tree, every species.

The following story shows how quickly the connection can happen when we are open to a new kind of relationship with nature. One day I was at an event where I had the opportunity to share some of the tree messages I had received with a few people in the group. A woman in her late 60s approached me, curious about this person who was talking about trees and receiving messages from them. Despite being in financial hardship she was inspired to purchase my collection of messages from the trees and off she went. Weeks later I was speaking at spiritualist church and saw her in the audience. She came up to me after the gathering with a beautiful letter she had written for me. She didn't have my address when she wrote the letter and had no idea how to find me to deliver it. Then, as synchronicity would have it, a friend of hers, not knowing that there was any connection between the two of us, mentioned that I was going to be the speaker that night. She was delighted that the universe lined things up for us to meet again. Her letter came straight from the heart. She wanted me to know how much the messages from the trees had changed her world. I was deeply moved to learn that the tree conversations inspired her to connect with a small shrub that had just been planted near the entrance of the apartment complex where she lived. She noticed that it wasn't being watered regularly and she became its care taker, sneaking out at 5:30 in the morning to water it. (I assume she was shy about giving attention to the shrub that wasn't even her responsibility). The letter went on to explain that, as she was giving special attention to this small shrub, it started communicating with her! Before this time, talking to a plant was completely out of her awareness. My heart soared to learn how the messages from the trees were opening up her world and leading to her own, heart-felt conversations. The trees have so many blessings to share with us. As we open up to them, they open us up. Being the catalyst for this awakening fills my soul, for it tells me that we are indeed remembering what it is to be so connected to nature. The more of us who are remembering this ability, the more we will love and protect our environment. It's a beautiful win-win opportunity.

It has been a few years since I first offered my tree workshop. In that time, humanity has continued to awaken with the ever-rising frequency of the Earth. There is definitely a difference in the experiences people are having four years after my first tree workshops were offered. My recent foray into the forest with a small group of people was very exciting because I was the one being validated, as each person received beautiful teachings and support from the trees. Even participants who were a bit skeptical about it all, received wisdom from the trees.

One woman who participated said she felt that my presence opened up a 'receptive field' to communicate with the trees you could say, because the connection was not as strong when she returned by herself to the same trees a few days later. We all have a purpose in this world, based on natural abilities that we come in with. I know part of my mission at this time is to be leading humanity back to our connection with the Earth. In the next chapter I explain in more detail the methods I use in the workshop and offer the meditation I created so that you can have the benefit of the information to enhance your conversations with a tree. For now, I'll share some of what others have experienced after connecting with the trees.

As I mentioned earlier, most people who would be interested in going into the forest to communicate with trees already have a love of nature. However, that often means being active in the forest, like hiking or skiing. When I moved to the Rocky Mountains in Alberta I found the community was very oriented to the outdoors. People were always active – mountain climbing or hiking or racing down the slopes. What I felt they were missing was a true connection to the beauty that was around them. They were busy doing, instead of being present with their surroundings. We know from the research that they would be receiving benefits of being out in nature, regardless of their intention. However, for the stress reduction benefits, it is best to be more 'present' with your surroundings and slow down enough to notice all the nuances that the forest has to offer. I went hiking one day with a couple of women half my age. It was great to sit at the mountain top and feel that accomplishment, and yet, on the way up, I felt I was missing all the little gifts that the trail had to offer, not wanting to hold up my companions by stopping every five minutes to admire the subtleties of the plant life on the trail. The difference between being present in nature and being active in nature is the invitation that the workshop brings to people. Participants are asked to be in stillness and truly connect to the trees that surrounded them. It opens up a new awareness that many of them said they will continue to enjoy.

After I offered the introductory meditation and some of the research about trees, participants were invited to start by leaning against a tree to see what they felt. Everyone went to the same two trees so that we could compare what each was sensing from them, noticing any similarities, which helps confirm what people are experiencing. A few people felt the tree pulling them in – like a magnetic force. This happens when standing with your spine against the tree, leaning your head onto the trunk as well. It seems to create an instant connection between you and the tree. One person was reminded to be playful and the tree told her to draw inspiration from the dancing river that was flowing by (the tree was on the river bank). It seems we can look to nature as an example of what we choose to create in our lives. First Nations people certainly know this, using 'animal medicine' to understand their lives. Animal medicine is giving attention to the animals that appear to you in life, especially if it is an uncommon occurrence. For example, deer represent gentleness. When they appear, perhaps it is a reminder to be gentle with yourself or someone in your life. If I wanted to foster more playfulness in my life, I would call upon the medicine of otter. They are well known for their playful nature. The trees were offering this same wisdom in telling the person to use the dancing and delightful river energy as inspiration for play.

There were several young people who attended my most recent workshops. Most were in their twenties. They attended thanks to an invitation from my daughter. What they experienced made me wonder if this generation is more open to the less tangible aspects of life, including conversations with a tree. They were having powerful experiences. One said he could feel the tree healing him and opening his heart as well as grounding him. I could tell that he was deeply moved by the surprise connection he felt with the trees and the ability to communicate so deeply. It confirms that the conversations are not only on the mental level. Most participants had body feelings and emotions arising as well when they were connecting to the trees. Several participants were close to tears, or deeply moved, when sharing their experiences. One participant felt himself being pulled into an ocean of green (the colour of the heart chakra), and said it made him feel "present" and he felt that his body liked it very much. My experience is that our bodies can benefit greatly from leaning against a tree. The tree automatically knows what needs to be done. This participant also had a strong feeling from the tree of how much the trees enjoy having humans connect to them and how indeed it is a symbiotic relationship. He felt a deep reverence and appreciation from the tree. The trees have been serving us for so long, simply by being, that it seemed the tree appreciated being acknowledged as the participant was open to the communication that was happening and very receptive to the tree.

Another participant was well aware of his connection to the trees, having accessed nature wisdom before through plant medicine. He offered a surprising tidbit of information that he received from the trees. They told him that people always benefit by being in the forest, even when they're not aware of it. Of course, we know this from the forest bathing research. However, what he learned was that the trees often help people who enter the forest with a troubled mind. The trees will offer insight that the person will think came from within themselves, but was actually given to them by the trees. How wonderful is that? Not only does the forest support us physically, but we can solve our problems with their support without even trying. I know the trees do not expect or desire credit for this, yet it expresses another benefit of being in the forest. When we are troubled and need insight into a situation, we can walk among the trees and leave wiser than when we entered.

When I asked the Earth Walk participants what stood out for them in their experience of the workshop, they told me that it made them realize that nature is "alive and aware". That's a great description of the presence that is in nature. We all know it is alive. It's a new understanding for most that it is also aware. It reminds me of a childhood animation where the trees are watching us as we pass by – without the 'bad guy' lurking in the background. Imagine walking through the forest or a wooded trail knowing that every tree is aware of your presence, offering love and guidance as you pass by! This combination of alive and aware is so different from the technology that so many of us connect to today. Think of the hours a day spent on our phones, or in front of the TV, or on the computer. Technology is man-made. It does not hold the vitality of the natural world. It has no life force, and even though it seems to have intelligence, it does not have awareness. Nature, on the other hand, is created by the All That Is. It has beneficial properties, unlike the harmful electrical fields that our man-made technology emits.

Being in nature brings us back to our true nature. This came forward in Richard Louv's work as well. In a world where most of us put on a mask to fit in or be who we think others want or expect us to be, returning to one's true self can be a great release and relief. Certainly the trees love you not only as you are, but specifically because of who you are. That is unconditional love and it is what the trees have to offer us. Loving each one of us for unique qualities without comparison or the need to fit a certain standard offers more relief than many of us recognize. Some participants were told that if they are ever feeling alone, they can connect with a tree and talk to the trees because they are always listening. The trees have shared this with me as well. We may think, well a tree can't hug me or hold me, and I would offer an argument to that. Yes, a tree will not move its branches to reach out and give you a big hug, but the love that I have felt from the trees goes much deeper than what most humans exchange as feelings of love. It drops so deeply into the heart that, as I have said, I am moved to tears in experiencing it. We can experience affection from another person and never drop into that level of unconditional love.

Henrietta explained the state of being that will allow us to return to that level of love in this way:

Humanity needs to be flexible and accept the changes that you see all around you. It must happen. Resisting it will only make it more difficult. The more people can flow with what is, the easier their lives will be. We, the trees, would highly recommend walking among us to make this transition easier. For you see, we do not resist what is. We know what is unfolding on the Earth and we accept all that is. Because of this, we remain in the constant state of love and so being with us will allow you to feel that love. You will feel the harmony of no-resistance that is the trees. You will feel the stillness. By being in nature, you will allow yourselves to walk in this harmony as well. You will come to appreciate us more than you have in the past. You will look at us differently, for you will see the qualities of yourselves there. You will see our branches reaching into the heavens and see that you also desire to be connected to the All That Is. You will see our leaves flourishing and growing as spring moves into summer and you will see that you too feel more celebratory as summer approaches. You will see our branches reaching out to touch one another and you will appreciate those around you. By being among us you will find your own self. It is the stillness of being in nature that will bring you back to your own center.

Here's a message from George that expands on what they offer us:

I would like to tell you about the energies that a tree emits and how we connect to humans. When you walk by a tree, it knows that you are there and it sends out a field of Light or energy to you as you pass by. It is our role to be supportive to all of nature and so we do this to support you in your lives. We pull our energy from the All That Is the same way that you do. So, we can offer that energy to you. People who are particularly loving will receive a different energy than someone who has intent to harm. The point is that we respond to our environment and to the people in our environment. If you would like to receive supportive energies through the day, send your loving kindness and thoughts to the trees around you and they will send the same to you. Every time you see them or think of them, they will send loving energies to you. That is why people can live in seclusion in the woods for example, and feel so loved, without the need for human contact. As you know, humans can be very hurtful but you will not feel hurtful energies from a tree. By loving the trees in your surroundings, your surroundings will feel more loving to you. Your surroundings will feel more like your own little sanctuary as you relate to your trees.

The one who writes these words has fond memories as a teenager of her relationship with trees. They were her support. They are what got her through troubled times. She did not know the depth of it at the time, but she could feel their support and their love doing what they could to comfort her. Many of you, as you read this, will have similar memories. You dismiss them but in truth, it is the trees connecting with you and vice versa. So, we are sentinels of loving support for you.

Fortunately, we are all over the planet, each climate bringing forth different species. Oh the diversity of this beautiful Earth is genius. Please appreciate it. There is so much wisdom in the evolution of the natural world. And there is so much of your soul residing there. The more you connect with it the more you connect with yourself. The more you truly connect with the natural world, the more you realize all that you are. All the emptiness will be lifted from you as you connect more with the Earth. Even those of you who do not think that you have a strong connection to the Earth, if you would allow yourself to spend more time in nature, you will find that you are more relaxed and just a little more content with the world. It is like therapy, being in nature – free, affordable, convenient therapy. Why not give it a try?

Good question indeed. As noted earlier, research is showing that it is not only physical benefits that we receive from being in nature. We also benefit mentally, emotionally and spiritually.

Earth Walk participants have also received the message that the trees come together as a group to offer healing to humans who walk among them. The trees stand as individuals, as the workshop attendees realized, offering support in their own unique way, and also join together, in a sense, to offer group support. The trees also shared that, once someone connects with them in person, they can make the same connection later on without having to be present in the forest. This was also told to me by the trees. Henrietta let me know that I can always connect with her, regardless of where I am. This makes sense if we accept that we are accessing information and memories from 'the field' where there is access to all.

I have learned from my forays into the forest with others that the trees are indeed our teachers, even when we don't realize we are being taught! Part of their purpose in being here is not only to support the great diversity of life that lives in, on, or near the trees, but to support us humans as well. A few years ago I was zip-lining while still living in Nova Scotia. After our adventures of flying from tree to tree we were led to a small shack to remove our gear. As I was unharnessing myself, I looked up and there was a National Geographic centerfold photograph of 'The President' – a giant sequoia tree in California. It is the second largest tree on Earth according to National Geographic. It stands at 247 feet tall and is estimated to be 3,200 years old! Being me, I again found myself in tears the second I caught sight of it. Why I have these visceral experiences of such incredible appreciation for trees is still unknown to me. What I do know is that I want to meet that tree!

Years after that experience of seeing 'The President', as I write these words, I am sitting on a beach on Vancouver Island. It is my new home as of a few weeks ago. One of the great blessings of being here is the ancient trees. To look up the trunk of a 350 year-old cedar, for me, is a humbling experience. I am immediately pulled into the awareness that the tree's experience of life is far beyond my short human journey. It leaves no doubt in my mind that the trees have unconditional love to share, for I am moved just by being in their presence. When I think of what it means to be a master – to hold wisdom garnered from years of stillness – it reminds me of what I feel from these trees.

The trees can be our teachers if we allow ourselves to recognize the presence that is tree. When we realize, as I have learned from the trees and other people, that they support us with insight, love, guidance, energy, cleansing, and wisdom, we are on our way home, for the trees are in our experience for a reason. They are part of this beautiful planet that we inhabit. They respond to the world very much as we do. They are grateful for our presence, for they know, more than we do it seems, what we have to offer just by being here. The more we pay attention and realize that all is connected, the sooner we will return to our magnificence as demonstrated by the trees. The great teachers are the ones who teach by example. They live their wisdom, ready to share with those who have the insight to ask. The trees have been holding ground on this Earth, some for centuries, waiting for our awareness to return, waiting to be asked, and then they joyfully respond, for they have so much to share.

It moves my soul to know that we are on our way back – back to the wisdom and guidance that comes from nature. In our return we will come to honour the land once again. And, as we honour the land we will soon find that we are honouring each other and, ultimately, ourselves. As I move along in my journey I find myself ever closer to the most ancient of trees – the giant sequoia of California. Although I did not recognize it as an intention, I see now that there are no mistakes. My willingness to move, and move, and move again has led me ever closer to my new teachers – the gentle giants that inhabit the west coast. I see now that they have been calling me. At this point I can only imagine the awe and admiration I will feel being in a forest full of those incredible Beings called the giant sequoia. It is an adventure I anticipate with great delight.

When I moved from Nova Scotia to Alberta the trees told me they had been waiting for me. Perhaps this message from George holds the explanation of why they were waiting. They are happy to know that their wisdom will be shared.

I am delighted to have this opportunity to speak through you today to all those who will read these words. We, the trees, are delighted that we can speak to so many through Jane. We carry wisdom that is seldom recognized. We understand the way of the natural world. We witness the way of the human, in your state of being disconnected from the natural world around you and we have less understanding of that. It makes us sad, you could say, that humans do not fully accept the opportunity to use trees for their benefit. For you see, not only do we give you oxygen to breathe, but we give you energy. There is a great energy exchange between humans and trees. We have the ability to turn the energy of the sun into green growth. Humans do not use the sun in this way, and so the energy we give off in that process benefits you. This has not been studied before, for no one has thought to do so. We invite your scientists to study the energy that is transmitted off of trees and how it is of benefit to humans. There is an exchange in this way as well. (This is not a reference to the phytochemicals that benefits us). *We can support you, and we do, but you are not aware of our support. It is why people feel so good when they live among the trees. Humans also need sunlight, so it is not good to allow the trees to keep you constantly in the shadows, but it is good to have trees around you. In your cities trees are planted to beautify and to make people feel better about where they live. We are an essential part of the human experience. The energy we give off is life-giving, just as oxygen is. We can support your life force with our life force. We stand tall and gather the life force energy of the Earth and the sun. With our ability to do this, we have much to offer to you as well. Touch a tree and you can feel this energy run through you.*

This is one way in which humans can benefit from being more connected to nature. You are, but you have forgotten. With this wisdom coming forward, you will develop more understanding about the symbiotic relationship that we have. You support us and we support you. Nature has many systems which function in this way. It is the way of harmony. It is the way of the natural world. Even as you see animals killing for their survival, as humans do, know that it is a harmonious relationship even though it ends with death for some. Nature knows that balance must be maintained for the highest benefit of all. However, in the natural systems, much of this balance is voluntary. Many species produce young in accordance with the availability of food. There is a natural respect for the environment and young are not brought into the world where there will not be enough to sustain them. Species other than humans respect the balance that is required for the sustenance of all. Humans, however, think only of their place in this hierarchy and do not consider the needs of those lower on the food chain. Humans do not even consider the need for balance. Much of what you do is out of balance. You find a nutritional substance that is beneficial and you isolate it from the source. You magnify its potency and use it that way instead of understanding that the food that originally contained the vitamin, or whatever the nutritional substance is, had many key components that allow the body to efficiently use the nutritional value of the substance. This is one example of how you are out of harmony with nature and now you are seeing your bodies very much out of balance, with many illnesses and emotional disturbances affecting humans at this time.

By finding your way back to the natural world and learning about how things work in nature, you will rediscover the truth of who you are as humans in relation to the Earth. There was a time when all lived in great harmony. It was a time when life was simple. There need not be technical advancements that lead you away from nature. You can use your technology to be in harmony with nature as well. It is the choices you make that lead you far from this balance. Come back to your source of life. It is like returning home after a long dispute. Find your way back to the natural world by being interested.

Come stand by a tree, touch the trunk and see what you feel. If nothing, that is OK. Send your love to the tree and know that it will be felt and returned to you ten-fold. Nature has a lot to give but it must be respected. All resources can be depleted when thrown out of balance. Humans have proven that. Look to nature for evidence of harmony and then ask where you can recreate that in your own lives. This would be good for humanity at this time.

I would like to end by saying that we are waiting. We are excited to think that humans will find their way back to nature through the trees. We are waiting.

A New Dawn

Let your tears fall.
Let them release and cleanse the patterns of the past.
A new dawn is awakening.
Be prepared.
Open your hearts to the Light
that it may restore your Radiance.
Open your throat to the song
that it may restore your Will.
Open your eyes to the heavens
that they may restore your Soul.
You are the Light.
You are Creator's song
in the heart of humanity.

CHAPTER SIX

The How and Why of Tree Talking

This chapter is for everyone who has been reading this book and thinking, "I want to do that!" Or, maybe you already communicate with trees, in your own unique way, and you are ready to expand your experience. What I am offering here are ideas and invitations to take your nature connection into a more heart-felt level. Please trust your own inner guidance if you receive ideas on how to connect that are different than mine. We each interpret the world through our own unique lens. My experiences with tree communicating will be different from yours because we all move through the world from the perspective of our individual nature and past experiences. It takes a lot of clarity to truly be in the moment without the influence of the past. Our subconscious is loaded with interpretations from our previous experiences that create the foundation of our beliefs. Those beliefs then create the base of our response to the world. For that reason, we shouldn't expect our experiences to be the same as anyone else's. Comparing ourselves to others is a set up for disappointment. I'm offering guidelines and ideas here but I encourage you to also trust what comes naturally to you in your intention to deepen your connection to the trees.

If your desire is to receive messages from trees, it's important to trust what comes to you and take every little tidbit you get as valid. Sometimes what we receive is so simple that we dismiss it. In fact, simplicity can be quite profound. When I teach my channeling workshop, people may get only one word yet, when given its proper consideration, that word could make a big change in their lives. The more you trust your abilities the more they will develop. Be positive, be patient and be playful with the intention to simply enjoy the experiences you are having. The lighter you can be, the easier it will be. By trusting your unique connection to the trees, you may discover ways of communicating that I haven't mentioned here. I see this book as an inspiration to lead you to your own beautiful expansion into the potential that a relationship with the trees has to offer.

Practice is an important step in expanding your skills. When Henrietta first reached out to me, I was also writing a channeled book at the time. That book is 350 pages long. I was sitting every day and connecting with the Higher Realms to receive those messages. I had a daily practice of channeling. It's very possible that this practice led me to a state of attunement that allowed me to hear that first invitation from Henrietta. Actually, I came to be writing the channeled book in the same way. I had a daily meditation practice and one day realized that I was being asked to be a scribe for the Council of Nine. The reason I bring this up is to make the connection between a disciplined practice and the success that we achieve. I have always found that my efforts of a dedicated practice have been rewarded.

Another important step is not to be discouraged if it seems that nothing is happening with the trees. When I first started practicing Reiki back in the mid-1990s, I couldn't feel the energy in my hands at all. I had to simply offer it out there and trust that it was working. In time, I became more sensitive to the energy and the channels opened up for me. Once it started, there were even times when I could feel the energy running through my hands when I had no intent of offering healing to anyone. I assumed, in those moments, that someone nearby needed some energy and I would just let it flow. Like anything, communicating with a tree may take practice. Have faith and trust that it will open up for you. And, the bonus is, whether you are aware of consciously communicating with a tree or not, you are going to receive the benefits of being among the trees. The forest bathing research is proof of that, so just keep playing with it and trusting that the more you do, the more it will open up for you. The trees have also made it very clear that we do not need to go to the forest only to receive messages. They give to us and also receive from us, regardless of our intent. The trees benefit from our presence just as we do theirs. It is a beautiful, symbiotic healing relationship that is beneficial in and of itself.

Fortunately, for those who have a burning desire to be in conversation with a tree, I believe the process is going to get easier as time goes on because we are now living in a higher vibration. This 'energetic soup' as the trees have described it, means that accessing our more intuitive skills and sensitive nature will be (and is) easier than it was in the past. The world is literally less dense so it is easier to connect to the finer energies of our environment. The greatest limitation that we now face is releasing our old beliefs about what is possible. I can easily speculate that many of you reading this book have been persecuted in past lives for expressing your witchy-poo abilities. I know from my work using the Freedom Release Technique in clearing limiting beliefs that many people hold an underlying fear of persecution for expressing their less 'normal' skills. I have done a lot of work for myself and others in order to feel safe in this lifetime in the full expression of our intuitive abilities. Other hidden fears that lurk deep in the subconscious are thoughts of being ridiculed, rejected, or considered mentally unstable. These fears are true limitations in allowing ourselves to move back into our intuitive nature as human beings. They often manifest as thoughts such as, "Oh, this is stupid. I'm not doing this any more - what was I thinking? Who am I trying to kid? Why would I want to talk to a tree anyway?" Maybe you don't want to talk to a tree and that's fine. But if, in reading this book, you did have the feeling that you want to be able to do the same, and those kind of thoughts come up for you, know it is your subconscious fears trying to protect you because of past experiences.

If you do recognize such fears, there are a variety of clearing modalities that you can use to help release them (see Teaching Moments at end of the chapter). Recognition is the first step in letting it go. You can then tell yourself that it is safe in these times to connect with trees. You can discern who to share your experiences with and when it is best to keep it to yourself. You are safe and you don't have to develop this ability over-night. If it takes two years, well, you have had two years of being among the trees and enjoying all the health benefits of doing so.

As stated earlier, I am quite sure that my ability to communicate with trees is related to past lives where I had a deep connection to nature. I would say it is also because of my personal make-up as a sensitive and an empath. I intuitively pick up on the energy of other people and no doubt, that led to such a deep connection with the trees as well. As we release our fears and become more accepting of our intuitive nature, humanity could quickly evolve into a level of normalcy regarding such abilities. After all, it is part of our animal nature. Wild creatures use these instincts all the time to avoid danger. If we were to develop our finer senses, we may also know when an Earthquake is about to happen or when we should wait just another minute at the traffic light because someone is about to run a red light. I have a friend who that happened to. She was driving and the light had turned green. Without knowing why, she paused and her husband, who was in the car with her, nudged her, saying the light was green. Just then a car went whipping by, having run the red light. Had she pulled out as soon as the light turned green, there would have been a serious accident. She didn't consciously know this would happen. Her hesitation came from an inner knowing that comes from the heart. That's why we should not rely solely on the mind for our understanding. HeartMath Institute has done studies on this and proven that the body (not the cognizant mind) knows what is about to be experienced a few seconds before an event happens. They believe this body knowing comes from the heart which has 40,000 brain cells in it. There is an instinctive nature to the heart that we have all but forgotten in our intellectual pursuits. Wisdom, I believe, is intellect balanced with heart intelligence. When we give credence to one over the other we are out of balance.

There is one fundamental requirement in receiving the most from your experiences with the trees and the tree community, or forest. You must be fully present with the experience of being in the woods or among the trees. No cell phones or ear buds if you want to truly connect with your surroundings. Even chatting with someone else distracts from the experience because it keeps you in your mind. This is not to say that you always have to go alone, but be sure to spend some time alone with the trees to enhance your experience. The joy for me is noticing every flower and the small insects or anything that rustles in the under-brush as I walk a wooded trail. I am alert to every song bird gifting me with its love tones. I am alive in the experience, awakening to a broader, peripheral sight and noticing what is around me. This, for me, is where the joy comes from. It is when I feel truly connected to the natural world around me and become one with it in a sense. Then my heart delights with the magic of the surprises that wait for me along the way. That is the true invitation – the joy. When you get into nature see it as an opportunity to get out of your mind. Then you are in a walking meditation without even trying and receiving all the benefits that meditation and the trees have to offer. Now, let's move into the many ways in which you can connect with the trees.

Give and You Shall Receive – How to Begin Conversations with a Tree

As you have learned in this book, when you give love to the trees they are happy to offer it back. Remember my experience walking down the city streets of Toronto. I wasn't trying to communicate with the trees at that time. I was simply in deep appreciation for everything around me, and visceral, unconditional love was given in return. You can do the same to begin your connection with a tree. The first thing I would suggest is to find a favourite tree near you and start sending it love every day. In my experience, trees do have different personalities and different roles to play. Make sure you choose a stately tree if you want to receive deep love and wisdom from it. Younger trees truly have a juvenile nature. If we were to compare it to channeling, I always call upon the highly evolved Beings of Light instead of opening myself up to any Being that wants to come along. Just because an entity from the other side connects with us doesn't mean that it is advanced and has something worthy to offer. The same is true with the trees. Be choosy.

Once you have found a tree that feels right to you, simply talk to it in your mind. Tell it how stately it is, how full and healthy it looks. Admire it. Discover its qualities and appreciate it. Maybe it has a strong trunk or a lot of leaves. Offer praise. I once said to a young oak how straight and tall it was growing and I got the sense that it felt like a young child that had just been praised. Put your hands on the trunk of the tree and give your loving energy to it. Be still in your mind as you do this, placing your focus on the tree, and see what you feel. Remember, if you feel nothing, that's OK. Just keep offering your love. After doing this for a while, put your back against the tree and see what happens. Again, empty your mind and notice what is happening in your body. Is your heart racing? Do you feel your breathing changing? Are you more relaxed? Does any part of your body experience a change?

The more you visit your tree the closer you will come to feeling a bond. Remember, this is not foolishness. Trees have a lot to give. I have felt their love so deeply that there is no denying that fact for me. And, if it's there for me, it's there for you too. Greet your tree whenever you visit. You can even project your thoughts to the tree and let it know when you're coming. Spend some time when you do visit, even if it's just sitting by your tree while you read or colour or do some journaling. The longer you are sitting in nature, the more benefits you are receiving and the longer those benefits will last.

Starting the Conversation

Let your mind play with this. Once you have established a 'relationship' with a tree you can start to take it to a deeper level.

There's nothing wrong with pretending that you and your new tree friend are having a great time together, unless you live too long in that world and forget to come back to 'reality'. Chat it up. Even if you are making up answers, it is a good exercise to get your imagination going. Remember what I learned from my work as a hypnotherapist, the mind does not know the difference between imagination and reality. If you are imagining it, then your mind thinks you really *are* having a conversation with a tree – and you are. In time you may come to find that what comes back is not really your own voice. That's why it's a good idea to have a journal for your visits. When you record the conversations you can begin to see when they change.

After doing this for a while, you might want to begin asking questions of your tree friend. We all have different ways of receiving answers. For some it may come in visual images that you can interpret. If you have faith that these images are in support of your question, then your interpretation can come from the place of trusting that the message has some benefit for you. For example, if you ask something about your health and you see an image of a gem stone, perhaps you might want to do some research on the qualities of that gemstone to see if it indeed holds healing properties related to your question. Other people may have a feeling in their body. Perhaps feeling more relaxed or yawning or sighing, which is a releasing. Others, like myself, may actually receive a message or a few words in response to their question. Whatever comes to you, don't immediately dismiss it. Just make note of it and let it sit with you. Also, don't expect the same experience the next time you visit your tree. This can be limiting. Your way of receiving answers may change, so try to be open each time to whatever the experience is that wants to come through. The important thing is to practice, practice, practice.

Pay attention to how you feel when you think of going to visit your tree. Do you feel some excitement at the thought? If so, it could be your tree sending a feeling to you, or at least the connection is deepening. There were times when I was on the trail to visit Henrietta and I could sense that she knew I was coming. One day, I was taking my daughter to 'meet' Henrietta. As we were walking along the trail I put my attention ahead to Henrietta and she said to me, "I see you are bringing your offspring to meet me." I started to tell my daughter but then felt so much love from Henrietta that I couldn't speak for a moment. I was on the verge of tears feeling the depth of her love. Another time George told me that he had been calling out to me for days, wanting to share a message with me. My belief is that the trees are here in service and that is what they want to do in whatever way that is for the tree and the area of the world it lives in. As I said, my relationship with Henrietta came to feel like a real human-like friendship. When the time came for me to move away from the area, I felt sad at the thought of not being able to be at her side and wondered what she felt about my leaving. She assured me that trees don't hold an emotional attachment. They accept what is in every moment. That helped me also accept the whole experience as a moment in my life, without feeling regret about moving. I will always have the treasure of the beautiful memories and messages that I have shared with you.

The thing that I would like to express the most to you is to let your imagination be real. Pretend that you are having a conversation with a tree. Make up the answers. My belief is that this is the place where we always create from. When we imagine, we are bringing reality into existence. I do a lot of work tapping into other realms of existence. For example, there is an energy vortex behind one of the mountains where I am living. One day

I decided to connect with that vortex. I was taken, in my 'imagination' on a journey. Weeks later, when I was sharing the experience with a friend, telling her about the message that came to me in that journey, I was moved to tears. The tears were a strong reaction that often happens to me when I am speaking a deep truth. Those tears helped validate for me, the message that I had been given from that experience. Even though the whole thing could be dismissed as my imagination, the fact that telling someone about it led to an instant reaction within myself that was so heart-felt that it brought tears, is enough to tell me that it is much more than an imaginary journey. I am telling you this so that you will validate your own experiences that may seem like you are just making something up. Be faithful in journaling your experiences. Then you can go back and read over what you have received at a later time when you can see it from a more objective state of mind. This will help you see that there may be something more happening than just your thoughts.

Please be aware, I am not suggesting that anyone live in the imagination versus 'reality' to a point of becoming unbalanced either mentally or emotionally. This is a very grounded experience and, even though you are using your imagination, at the same time you are very aware of your surroundings and your place on this Earth as well as being fully anchored in the physical body and the present moment. What I am offering as guidance is meant to enhance your experience in nature. It is your responsibility to use the information in a way that best meets your beliefs and abilities. It is important to be mentally balanced and aware of the 'normal' world, even when you are connecting to the trees.

Meditation in Preparation for Conversations with a Tree

As mentioned in the previous chapter, starting your connection to the trees with this meditation may contribute to more success with your tree conversations. You can print the meditation to use on location or simply remember the basic steps and expand on it when you are with the trees. I originally learned a version of this meditation from Drunvalo Melchizedek who has written several books on sacred geometry and other topics. It is a powerful way to start any meditation. You can use it to get into the heart and then move into your meditation. In this case, we use it to be sure that we are centered and focusing on the heart, where so much wisdom lies, before connecting to the trees. I recommend reading it over once before using it in meditation, so you are familiar with the steps before you actually use it on site.

Find a comfortable location near your tree of choice. Close your eyes and take a few deep breaths and bring all of your awareness into your body. Notice any muscles that are tight, or any feelings of discomfort. Let yourself relax and release any tension as you feel your body becoming heavier, feeling the Earth beneath you. In a moment you are going to move your focus from your mind and move it down toward your heart. Imagine that your awareness is like a mini version of you, standing behind your eyes, looking out to the world. You are going to take that mini-you and move it down to your heart. Imagine now that mini-you is turning around to face the back of your head and pretend what it would be like to be seeing the inside of your skull. Notice the curved shape of the back of your head. Now you are going to slide down that curve into your throat. You can be playful with this. Feel how slippery it is in your throat and how warm it is. Imagine you are looking out from under your chin now. You have the sense that your chin is above you as you look out from your throat. The idea is to really put your awareness in this part of your body and out of the mind. Now slide further down and imagine you are landing on top of your heart. The little mini-you may have trouble standing on your heart as it beats and pulses. You can have fun here and see yourself trying to hold your balance.

In a moment you are going to jump off your heart and imagine a spiraling vortex at the back of your heart that pulls you right into your heart. Once you get inside the heart you are going to land in a small room that is your special place. Imagine yourself now jumping up and being pulled into that vortex. See yourself spiraling, then landing in that small room in your heart. If it is dark, ask that there be light in your room. Use your creativity to pretend, see, or sense what your special room looks like. Is there colour there? What are the walls like? If nothing is coming to you, make it up. Tell yourself the walls are white and it is warm in here. In the beginning you may need to make it up and that will get you started. If it stays dark, that's OK. Practice many times until you find that there is light when you request it.

Once you have familiarized yourself with your special room, imagine there is a doorway. Notice what it looks like. Perhaps it is round with two doors opening out from the center. Perhaps it is like a draw bridge. Whatever comes to you, allow that to be your door. As you put your attention on the door it opens by itself and beyond the door is a brilliant, sparkling light. It is very bright and yet it doesn't hurt your eyes. You step out into the light and as you do you feel deep love, as if the Light is love itself. The Light then begins to fade. Now you can see before you, a large oak. You feel great presence in this tree. You say hello to it and connect with it in your imagination. You feel this mighty oak sending love to you and joy that you have chosen to communicate with it. You can let this tree talk to you now or you can ask the oak to help you connect with the tree that you have chosen to have a conversation with. Tell it that you are here to create a relationship with your chosen tree, and see what you sense coming back from the mighty oak.

Stay in the meditation as long as you like, connecting with the oak. When you are ready to open your eyes and connect with your tree for real, simply tell the oak that is what you are going to do. Keep the heart space open as you lean against your chosen tree with your spine along the trunk. Be with your tree in person for as long as you like. When you are finished communicating with your chosen tree, say good-bye in whatever manner works for you. You may want to record what happened in your body or any message or feelings you have about the experience. Then, when you are completely finished communicating and connecting with your tree, consciously see yourself go back to the mighty oak in your heart. Thank the oak for its wisdom and guidance. See the door close behind you as you enter back into the small room in your heart. Move mini-you from the heart, back up through the throat and into the head once again. Position yourself behind your eyes, as if placing yourself to look out from your physical eyes once again. Then bring your energy field back closer to your body with the intent of being balanced in all your chakras and ready to connect to the outside world once again.

If you feel light headed or ungrounded after your experience, put your bare hands or bare feet on the ground. You can imagine roots coming up from the Earth to hold onto your ankles and bring you back to the Earth. Remember to be playful with this. Make it a fun, joyful activity and allow it to be whatever it is. Expectation creates disappointment. If you arrive at this activity with an open mind, trusting whatever happens is just the right experience for you, then you will enjoy it more and you will allow each tree conversation to be unique. You can also submit any questions to info@conversationswithatree.com.

This information should give you a good start on how to communicate with a tree if that is your interest. However, as we have learned from the trees, we don't need to consciously communicate with them. We are benefitting from the trees and them from us, with our presence in the woods. Aside from communicating with the trees, they also offer powerful healing. As we have learned, they help us work through our troubles without us even knowing. And, I am reminded of another benefit in this message from Henrietta:

Trees are love – love expressing through existence – creating a symbiotic harmony with you humans. If you want to know how to BE love, make friends with a tree. The tree will share all of itself with you. It will bless your aura and cleanse it for you. It will scan your emotional field and clear it for you if you ask. Use your imagination and believe it is possible. (In that moment I asked for a scan. Henrietta did an emotional scan. I clearly felt releases in my neck, high heart, and lower abdomen. It was powerful and incredible to think that a tree could do this for me! As if to respond to my thought, Henrietta went on...) *This is what love can do and this is what love truly is – giving from a place of fullness. There is no emptiness when you are full of love. Everything feels blessed and beautiful. That is the way existence was meant to be on this planet. We hope to be here to see it restored. It is awakening now. How well it is nurtured will indicate its growth. Like sunlight and rain for all plant life – loving humans will restore the Earth.*

Here's a little bit more about the benefits of being with trees that don't relate specifically to conversations.

Healing from the Trees

We know from the research that just being among the trees is beneficial. You can also be more specific and ask your tree for healing, as we just learned in that message from Henrietta. When you lean against the tree with your spine along the trunk, lots of healing can happen. I once did this with a young elm tree. Young is a relative term here, as it was very tall. The moment I was leaning back against the tree my heart started pounding. It was so intense that I wasn't sure I would be able to stay with it. I had to breathe deeply to manage the energy that was running through me. It reminded me of the breathing exercises I learned in prenatal training. I asked the tree what the heck was happening and it answered me with a question. It asked, "How many days has it been since you have *not* had a cup of coffee?" I had given up coffee for almost 20 years, before taking it up again. Apparently it wasn't the healthiest thing for my body. The tree was clearing my body of the effects. Another time I leaned against a huge ancient cedar in the interior of British Columbia, Canada and had the same, intense heart pumping experience. This time I was told that the tree was clearing electro-magnetic energy from my body. At the time I was living close to a power station. It said that it was clearing my blood. I stayed for about ten minutes before moving on even though effects of the clearing were still happening. This tells me that the healing effects of trees are beyond what researchers have confirmed for us. Not only do they offer the effects that forest bathing researchers have discovered, I believe they can do much more. Of course, the messages from the trees are also healing because they are leading us to a more peaceful existence. In truth, what could be more healing than living a life of peace?

Whatever you have happening in your body, or emotionally, that could use some healing, take it to a tree. Lean against a tall, stately tree and ask it to offer you healing. Others who have participated in tree workshops have been told that we can receive the benefits from the trees just by being under the canopy of the tree, without actually leaning against it. I do not doubt this, yet I recommend your spine against the tree with your head resting on it as well, to have a more visceral experience in the beginning. I have also read that trees can reduce the effects of headaches. When you think about it, what is more grounded than a tree? Its roots spread far over the Earth and then connect with other roots that expand the connection even further. This grounding energy is very healing as I shared earlier. Added to that is the tree's ability to access the All That Is that may well be adding to the healing benefits. After all, I didn't ask the tree to heal my coffee intake or the electrical energy in my body but the trees knew to do that for me. Perhaps the wisest thing would be to ask the tree to offer whatever you need most and trust that it will know what that is.

Tree Talking with Children

We all know that children have vivid imaginations. They live in a different world than adults do, in a sense, because their state of being is not as cognizant as ours. The ability to reason doesn't develop until around the age of eight. Before then, children are in a lower brain wave state that benefits from play and imagination. Developing creativity and imagination is vital in these times when technology is so much a part of our lives. The technology we use and how we use it creates brain patterns in children that diminish the ability to focus. The Earth offers a very 'natural' way to balance that. Children quickly learn to create their own play in the forest. Even as children move into their early teens, the idea of building a fort or teepee out of sticks and materials they find in the forest, is a creative endeavour that holds their interest and brings all the health benefits of being in the woods.

The invitation for children is not necessarily to talk to trees, but to become at home in the woods and experience all the wonder and magic that the environment offers. Developing a love of the land at a young age will offer a lifetime solution to managing stress. And, as studies have shown, being in nature is very beneficial for all children. For children with ADHD forest bathing has been shown to match the benefits of Ritalin. Pure, natural healing that is free for the enjoying. Following are a variety of ideas to make your forest walks a creative adventure for you and your young ones.

Name that Tree

This may require some homework for the adults. Whether you are going to a nearby park, down your street, or into the forest, ask your children how many trees they can identify. Take pictures of the ones that you don't know and make it a research project to find out what the unknowns are. You may identify them by the bark, the leaves, or your geographic location for example. This is a great opportunity to teach children that different latitudes and altitudes support different types of trees. You can explain the difference between coniferous and deciduous trees. You can collect leaves from trees to take home to use as research. You can explain the different uses of hardwood and softwood trees. Some trees are preferred for building fine furniture or housing materials because of their colour or grain. Birds eye maple is appreciated for the small dots in the lumbered wood. Pine is easy to work with and would be suitable for carving. There are many properties of trees that you can use for your exploration. Some trees may have moss hanging off them. Some may have fungus that is specific to the tree species. For example, birch trees are host to a fungus that is good for making tea and holds many healing properties. By doing some research, or using your trip as an exploration to discover what you don't know, you can come up with lots of ideas to make it an interesting and educational outing.

Bring the Magic Alive

What is even more fun for children is to find magic in the woods. Maybe it's a wee hole under a root where you can try to guess what lives there. Is it a mole or a rabbit hole? Teach your children to notice all the nuances of the trees – what their bark is like – what is growing on the forest floor – how far the roots spread – if there are any wee toadstools growing nearby. What plants like to grow in the shade of the trees? Are there pine or spruce needles under the trees? What could you do with some of the sticks and leaves that you find in the forest? Your children will easily find the magic in the forest if you allow them to lead the play. Engage in their world and let them teach you with their vivid imaginations. They live in a world that still holds magic – free of the burdens of responsibility. Meeting them there will offer a reprieve from your daily concerns as you move out of the mind and into the moment. Perhaps the fairy kingdom wants to come alive and be part of the magic. Explore according to your values while embracing the wonder that children bring into the world.

Noticing Life Cycles

As you return to a deeper connection with the Earth, begin to be more observant of the cycles of nature and how they relate to your own life cycle. As the days shorten, what do you notice in the vegetation around you? Are deciduous trees losing their leaves? Are there more coniferous needles in the undergrowth? Is the undergrowth dying off? How do you feel at these times? Do you feel tired earlier when the days are shorter? Could it be an invitation to slow down, just like the natural environment around you is?

If you live in more tropical climates notice the stage of fruit-bearing trees. Are they in bloom? Ask your children what happens when the flowers fade? Do you have wet and dry seasons? How does the environment change in those seasons? How do these seasons affect your mood? When we teach children to recognize these cycles in nature in relation to themselves, we are creating self-awareness. I believe that self-awareness is a beautiful gift. The more we know ourselves, the more we can take care of ourselves in a way that is healthiest for us. We are not all the same, and the more we recognize and honour each person for their unique manner of being in the world, the happier we will be individually and as a whole. Self-realization supports that. There is no questioning that the environment and the cycles of nature affect us. One day I was driving in the city and I could sense a frantic energy on the road and knew I had to be extra alert as I was driving. When I wondered what it was about I realized that Mercury was coming out of retrograde that day. There is no doubt in my mind that it was that planetary motion that was affecting the mood of the drivers. The full moon is one example that most people can relate to. The beauty of using the trees and the forest to identify these cycles is that it is unfolding in front of us. We can *see* the changes happening and use them to teach our children of the cycles of life.

Bugs, Bugs, Bugs

It's easy as a parent to pass off our fears onto our children. For some people, the thought of appreciating bugs is repulsive. And yet, why go through life being afraid of bugs? After all, we're A LOT bigger than they are. Yes, some can do harm and that's another reason to notice bugs. The more we become aware of our environment, and notice everything that moves, the less likely we are to be harmed. We become alert and aware as more of our instinctive nature comes alive. Some of the greatest wonders of being in the forest are on the ground or close to it. Lift some leaves or rocks and you will find many creepy crawlies living there. In Canada we have very few insects that are harmful so this is a safe activity. Depending on your location of course, it is important to know what to look for and what to be careful of. That awareness itself is valuable information for children. I was tending my flower garden one day and had coreopsis flowers growing there. They are a yellow, daisy-like flower. Something drew my eye into the center of one of the flowers and there was a large bumble bee but it wasn't moving. When I looked closer I realized the bee had been captured by a comparatively small, yellow spider. It was fascinating. The spider was a fraction of the size of its prey. Being yellow, it had the perfect camouflage to capture its victim. The two front legs of the spider were holding onto the bee. Undoubtedly the spider had injected some venom that allowed it to tame the buzzing bee. From then on, I was aware of these spiders when doing my gardening. I didn't want to experience that bite even though it wouldn't cause any serious harm to me.

Children are often fascinated with bugs and familiarity with them is beneficial. It's good to know what is harmless and what to be wary of without generating fear. Bugs have an important role to play in maintaining ecosystems. They eat other dead insects or eat insects that cause harm to plants. They burrow and aerate the ground. They live in the bark of trees or under their leaves. They are also a part of the ecosystem that is tree. As we know, trees can be home to birds, squirrels and even raccoons. The birds feed off the bugs that may be crawling on the bark and that is another way to get children to truly notice their environment. How many different kinds of bugs do they see? Where are they – on the ground, in a tree? What kinds of spiders do you see on your walk? Do they have webs or live in a hole in the ground? Can you find one that is making a web? Do they jump? Let the children lead the activity as you become keenly aware of the incredible world of bugs.

Edibles or Deadibles?

Nature foraging is another fascinating discovery for children and adults. Again, it's good for them to know what might look like a yummy berry or 'mushroom' could be poisonous. When you're in the forest there are plants and mushrooms that are edible. In North America for example, we can gather rose hips in the fall for tea that is rich in vitamin C. In the spring we can pick the tips of the new growth on the spruce trees for a refreshing tea with many health benefits. What we learn as children often stays with us all our lives. Knowing how to identify what to eat and what not to eat when in the forest is valuable information that may just be needed some day.

I was excited one day on a walk on a new trail when I found some orange mushrooms in the woods that looked like chantrelles. Since no one had ever identified them for me, I picked a couple and then went home and did some research. What I found interesting was that there can often be safe and poisonous mushrooms living within close vicinity of each other. I inspected my chanterelles and found that they met all the requirements of the authentic, edible mushroom. When I went back I also saw the imposters growing nearby which validated the need to be very cautious before consuming food that we have foraged. However, once positively identified, it can be satisfying to know that you can safely harvest your own food from the forest. It doesn't get much fresher or more organic than gathering part of your dinner from the woods on the way home.

Just a note to add to the foraging fun, I like to always leave some behind to be sure that whatever I am picking will proliferate and continue to grow in that area. If you are fortunate to have berries growing such as raspberries, blueberries or strawberries, you know they are easy to identify and it can be delightful to pick and eat right there in the woods. Please also be aware of plants that are on the endangered list so that you're not picking the last precious few specimens. One example of such a plant is the lady slipper that grows wild in Nova Scotia forests. It's a type of orchid that is close to extinction. It's always such a treat to see them in the spring and to know that they are to be enjoyed only on my walks and not from a vase on the kitchen table. It makes the joy of finding them that much more meaningful.

When we lived on the property that we moved to when I was twelve we had wild strawberries and blueberries growing in the meadow right beside the house. My mother thought it was the best thing ever to enjoy strawberry shortcake made with those wild berries. I would have thought so too if my sister and I weren't in charge of the picking! Wild strawberries are about the size of a small pea. It seemed like it took all day to fill a bowl full but I have to admit that the shortcake tasted like none other. Today we are so disconnected from the source of our food that these activities will develop a new appreciation of what we eat, how fresh it is and how close to home it was grown. I have read that food that is grown in our local area contains properties from the soil that can help reduce environmental allergies. This makes sense to me based on my understanding of natural therapy. I won't expand on that here but I invite you to do some research if you are interested.

This chapter offers many ideas and methods to connect more with the natural world around you and with trees in particular. The rewards are yours to experience. Pay attention to how you feel before entering the forest and after you have spent some time there. Do you feel more relaxed after your foray among the trees? Have you received any insight about your life? The more you notice, the more you will see the rewards and benefits that you are gifting yourself with and your loved ones. As Henrietta has suggested, get out of the mall and into the forest and your life will feel more blessed and less stressed.

Teaching Moment

If you are interested in doing some clearing work to release limiting beliefs and patterns from your life, you can go to my website: www.rashana.ca (Rashana is my Spirit Name and was my legal name for 9 years). There you will find a link for the Freedom Release Technique and another link that leads to www.freedomreleasetechnique.com.

My work with the Freedom Release Technique (not to be confused with EFT, or the Emotional Freedom Technique, which is the tapping technique) is unique to each person and may include soul retrieval, Akashic records reading and mediumship. You will find more information on the websites mentioned.

Be a Beacon

*Oh let your hearts sing as you feel
The new energies of the Earth.
The time of awakening is upon you.
Act now and join the celebration.
Give up the illusions of difficulty and strife.
Pass away the denial of the Self.*

*Nothing is more beautiful
Than a Soul awakening to the truth.
You are Creator in human form.
Recognize your Light
And make the world shine.*

CHAPTER SEVEN

New Humans on a New Earth

As I come to the final chapter of this book I am deeply aware that it is not an ending but a whole new beginning. Several years after my first conversation with a tree I find myself in another state of deep transition and transformation. I have moved from one side of the continent to the other – from the Atlantic Ocean to the Pacific. It is a symbol of the great divide I feel between who I am now and who I was when Henrietta first reached out to me. I never could have imagined what was in store for me then. Talking to trees has been one of the most beautiful experiences of my life. They have loved me and guided me and continue to support me. And yet, with every transition, I realize I am being invited into what else is possible. If trees have so much wisdom to share, why not the mountains and the rivers, or this beautiful ocean crashing to shore beside me as I write? What else is possible in this connection with the Divine through nature?

In my continual journey of change and transformation, I have come to realize that everything comes in perfect timing. The fact that this profound connection with the natural realm is awakening within me so deeply at this time, tells me that it is available to all of humanity. Only as I put these thoughts to paper now do I see the significance of the year 2012, when we passed that great marker into a new 26,000-year cycle, being the year when I first found myself in conversation with a tree, as if it is a symbol of what is to come. Just as I recognize a great transition in my life, so too is all life moving into a new phase of evolution. We are part of a living, breathing system. As we connect more fully to it, we also awaken the fullness of our human capacity and expression.

My conversations with the trees have shown me beyond any doubt that our connection to the natural world is deeper than we have believed in our recent history. The indigenous people of most nations have kept it alive, yet often hidden from the greater population who did not have the understanding and appreciation to honour their traditions. As one who lived without any education of the traditions of my ancestors, I am aware of the void we carry with the lack of it. For most of my life, I held a great reverence for the land without any cultural awareness to anchor it to. I had no concept of the significance of that void until about a year before leaving Nova Scotia. I attended a workshop facilitated by a powerful man from Ireland who is deeply connected to his ancestry and the traditions of the Druids. As we were gathered in the rural home of our hosts, the sun came streaming through the window, casting shadows on the floor into the center of our circle. The facilitator said something then that made me feel like I had come home to myself. In paraphrasing he said, "You see those shadows on the floor? That is not just light and shadow. In our tradition that is sacred." Something came alive in me when I heard those words. In that moment, it felt like he understood me more than I knew myself. Finally, I was given a foundation for the deep reverence I have felt at the sight of dancing shadows on the wall as sunlight came streaming into a room, or onto the forest floor. It has always stirred some unknown wonder within me, and my heart would dance with delight at the sight of it. All my life I felt alone in that appreciation. Never had I heard anyone speak of the sacredness of the shadows. To learn that Druids, who would have been my blood line, honour the shadows cast by the light affirmed some great tradition that, no doubt, I have lived in past lives. It is arising within me once again, leading me to this deep and profound connection with the trees and a sense of wonder about what else is possible.

While still living in Nova Scotia I found a curiosity awakening within me to connect more deeply with the world of nature that surrounds us. I was living in a small coastal community and would often go for a walk to a tiny, inhabited island that was linked to the mainland by a short, narrow road. At the end of the island was a vacant lot with two large boulders near the entrance. These huge rocks were about four feet tall and six feet wide and stood out in the landscape, as though they had been dropped out of the sky. I was no longer living near Henrietta and George and didn't find any trees that really called out to me. Perhaps that lack of connection to a particular tree was what encouraged me to explore and connect with one of the boulders. Both boulders are granite rock which is common in Nova Scotia. I remember as a child that granite was my favourite rock because it sparkled with the pieces of quartz crystal that makes up a large part of its form. I walked over to the one closest to the road, acknowledge it by saying hello in my mind, and placed my hands upon it. Within seconds I found myself floating in space, whirling through the dark void on the way to Earth. The rock was showing me its journey to planet Earth. It told me that it (meaning it and others like it) was responsible for inhabiting the Earth with microbial life as comets came falling out of the sky eons ago. It was showing me that it has been here since the beginning you could say. This was a completely different experience from connecting to the trees. The trees offer guidance, love, wisdom and seem to be here to support humanity in our return to love. The boulder, on the other hand, was taking me back in time. I had a sense of the Earth in the very early stages of the evolution of life.

To affirm the possibility of comets bringing life to our planet, I did a quick search online and found that a study conducted by Dr. Haruna Sugahara, from the Japan Agency for Marine-Earth Science and Technology, and Dr. Koichi Mimura, from Nagoya University in Japan. Their research "…indicates that comet impacts almost certainly played an important role in delivering the seeds of life to the early Earth…" The source of this information also noted that "When NASA's Deep Impact spacecraft crashed into Comet Tempel 1 in 2005, it discovered a mixture of organic and clay particles inside the comet. One theory about the origins of life is that clay particles act as a catalyst, allowing simple organic molecules to get arranged into more and more complex structures." Again, it is satisfying to have scientific theory support the information I receive from the organic life I connect to. I know now that even though rock is inanimate, it is not void of life and 'intelligence'. [11]

No doubt the intelligence of the boulder that chose to share that vision with me is the intelligence that directs all organic life. Like my tree friends, the boulder also helped me with my daily life. One day I was visiting and it reminded me of something I had to do later on that I had completely forgotten about and would have missed if not reminded by the boulder. I also sensed that the huge rock had a more feminine energy whereas the other similar boulder nearby felt more masculine to me. For some reason, I had not approached the masculine boulder until after a few visits with the feminine one. Perhaps that was an intuitive knowing, because the day I did decide to go place my hands on the masculine boulder it asked me not to touch it. I was taken aback at first, feeling rejected. It explained to me that it was placed very near a power pole, and therefore a great deal of electricity was running through it that would not be good for my body. Because it is surrounded by trees, I hadn't even noticed the power pole until then. Being made of granite, the boulders certainly would be good conductors. I was grateful that the rock honoured me with that warning.

My introduction to rock energy started in Nova Scotia, on the east coast, and expanded as I moved west. As part of my journey to the Pacific Coast, I lived for six months in the Rocky Mountains in Alberta, Canada, to be closer to my children. There I became curious and ready to expand my connection to the land that I called home. A healer in the town informed me that there is a major energy vortex in one of the mountains nearby that is known in the Vedic tradition to be the crown chakra of Mother Earth. To be living in the energies of that vortex was very exciting. I knew the area was sacred because Lake Louise, only a few kilometers away, is Archangel Michael's home base on the Earth you could say. However, the information about the crown chakra vortex was completely new to me. Once the days became warmer and spring invited me to be outdoors more often, I decided to explore the possibility of connecting to rock nature again. Since I was living in such a powerful part of the world, in the beautiful Rocky Mountains, why not take advantage of the location and have a conversation with a mountain?

My first attempt was with a piece of rock that had fallen off the side of a mountain face that was along a creek where I was hiking with a friend. I took it home, hoping to be able to connect with the mountain energy through the piece of rock that had fallen off. That proved to be fruitless as I received nothing from the rock. I guess it would be like trying to connect with a tree by using a stick. I never tried it, since the trees were so readily available. Still being curious about what a mountain may have to share, I wasn't ready to give up. I decided to go to my familiar nature connection and ask a tree about the potential of connecting with the mountains. Outside the condo where I was living stood a cluster of tall fir trees. I chose the biggest one to have a conversation with. It was right outside my bedroom window and had been attracting my attention since I moved there. Perhaps it had been waiting for me to connect. The tree calls itself Henry. I asked him how the energy of trees compares to mountains and was told that trees are more active than mountains because of their roots. Henry stated that, above ground, trees appear very still but a lot happens along the trunk of the tree, under the bark and in their roots as we know. *"Mountains, of course, do not have the same energy connection, although they often have veins of metals or other energy channels running through them. Mountains hold more Earth energy versus the energy that comes from the sun that feeds most life."* Henry added something that really caught my attention. He said *"When water runs through the mountains you are receiving telluric energy from the water."* That was exciting to me since I had started drinking water from a spring in the town. What a blessing it was to have a fresh, never-ending supply of pure, crystal clear, naturally filtered water pouring out of the base of a mountain! I felt so fortunate to have this precious, life-giving resource so close. Although not a lot of people took advantage of it, some residents from the nearby city would drive an hour to gather it. And here was Henry talking about telluric energy in the water. Telluric energy is low frequency electric currents that travel the Earth's crust. This seems to be the energy that feeds mountains as opposed to the direct benefit of sunlight. Telluric energy is influenced by solar wind and the geomagnetic activity of the Earth. It would make sense that water would conduct this energy. It may also describe some health benefits of naturally sourced water that we haven't yet recognized. After all, when we ingest the water, that Earth resonance would affect our body frequency to be more in tune with it. In contrast, when water passes through narrow pipes, at sharp angles, the structure of the water changes. Some claim that water travelling through taps is basically dead. It loses its healthy structure with the unnatural movement around sharp, 90-degree corners as it flows from pipe to pipe. Compare this to natural water channels that move through gentle curves or slowly trickle through the Earth to reach the base of the mountain. That water (aside from any pollution that may be affecting it) is very much alive.

After the surprise of learning what Henry had to share about telluric energy in the water, I went back to my purpose in asking about having a chat with a mountain. He told me that conversations would be less 'alive' than talking to trees because of the way in which we need the sun. My sense was that the veins of ore that run through mountains are a source of life, or Earth energy, for mountains, versus direct sunlight, which is the source of life for the plant and animal kingdom that we are a part of. It makes sense. If the sun were to be obstructed by clouds for a year, most plant life would die, which would then lead to the demise of almost all life on the planet. However, mountains and minerals would remain unaffected, or at least be less affected.

After my unsuccessful attempt to garner something from the rock that had eroded from the mountain, I decided to hike up into the woods across the street from where I was living and connect with the vortex I had been told about to see if I could talk to a mountain that way. While I was focusing on going within to still my mind, there was a very loud machine running nearby. It was distracting me as I was settling into my sunny location on the side of the mountain. Despite the irritation of the noise I did my best to ignore it as I went into my heart space in preparation for my journey. I imagined being invited into the vortex and this time the meditation seemed very real. It was a powerful experience about my purpose in being in that town. It seems with my deep connection to nature comes the invitation to be of service to the land. This I knew from past experiences, like clearing the land from the expulsion of the Acadians back in Nova Scotia. Perhaps this is why I have been such a wanderer in my life. However, something happened during that conversation that was also very affirming of my connection. After I settled myself, and the communication started, I was told that a time would soon come when we would no longer choose to create a world that included such loud machines as the one that had been chugging on as I was in meditation. In that instant, the noise stopped! It was split second timing! The moment I received the message was the moment the machine stopped. It left no doubt in my mind that this time I truly was connected and I was very grateful to be given that validation. However, that journey was more of a personal one and did not come from the mountain itself. I still had not found success having a conversation with a mountain.

Months after that experience and moving yet again to Vancouver Island, I decided to try one more time to see what a mountain might have to offer as rock solid wisdom. This time I was sitting on a beach near Victoria, looking across the water to

Mt. Baker, in the USA. It is part of the Olympic Mountain Range that rises up from the distant shore and provides a beautiful view from my Canadian vantage point. Mt. Baker stands above the rest and, in the summer months, is the only one that is snow capped. My child-self imagined it like the only frosted cupcake on the plate and, I had the sense it was open to connecting with me. This time I found success. Maybe it's a matter of finding the right mountain, just like finding the right tree to communicate with. Here's what Mt. Baker had to share:

Mountains are the Earth. We are not water on the Earth or trees growing on the Earth, we are the Earth – that which some call Terra Firma. We are unmovable, except by the Earth. (I questioned this thought of being unmovable …) You can break us down with your explosions but you cannot move mountains. We represent the past – Earth history. We represent 'what was' much more than 'what is'. Yes, you do see rock slides and erosion which represent a small part of what is. And yet, being as solid as we are, it is slow movement except in times of great upheaval. This is why many mountains hold powerful energies – because there is not as much change or movement and so memories and intentions can be firmly anchored in.

Humanity, on the other hand, is very different. You must change at this time. The longer you wait the harder it is for you and the Earth. There is a great call for awakening at this time that is facing much resistance. You are so firmly embedded in the past that you resist the urge for change. Humans cannot help but feel the need for change, for the energies are shifting. But, like the fear you face of looking within, many push the urges for change away. They do not recognize that it is an invitation into something more beautiful than has ever been on your planet. Yes, Jane, (a response to my question about the word 'ever') this is the potential – more wonderful than even Lemuria. But, you must begin to accept the urge to change – to release the past. You must resist the urge to repeat yesterday. You must let go of the fear that keeps you on the wheel.

"How do humans do that?"

You forget what was. You feel into the potential of what could be. You ask, 'What is the highest potential for me and this planet this day? Spirit, All That Is, show me the highest potential. Give me the eyes to see, the ears to listen, and the wisdom to accept the highest potential. Give me the heart for change and the mind for a new wisdom to reveal itself on this Earth.' You must ask for that which you desire. One problem is that people keep asking for the same thing. If it does not come, it is not in the highest and best for all. What more could you ask for? How can you expand your asking? How can your asking lead to your greatest purpose? Stop pretending to be small. The Earth is weary of this pretending. You are so much more than you allow yourselves to even imagine being. It is because many of you do not imagine. You do not think for yourselves. You look for someone else's science to make up your mind for you. Find your own science. Be your own Creator. Stage your own play that will be your life. That is all I have for you now.

There was my first message from a mountain. It felt like a little tough love mixed with wise counsel. The tone of the message was different than the more loving essence that comes through the trees, certainly stronger. It reminded me of times, when offering channeled sessions, that the Guides would be strong in what they offered. I know it happens when it is in the best interest for the person receiving to hear such a clear message. This message from Mt. Baker had a similar feeling. I decided to accept the advice to stage my own play and write out the scenes that I am choosing to be my future. If we are indeed the creators of our play that we call life, why not write the script and choose the actors? Then we can sit back and watch how it all unfolds. We can place ourselves in the audience and see how the chosen actors interpret their lines.

Having received that powerful message from a mountain, I was ready to connect with the Pacific Ocean. It has a different feeling from the wild energy of the Atlantic Ocean that surrounded my home province of Nova Scotia. The Pacific feels lighter to me, as if it holds a less dense energy of the experiences of humanity. I was curious to see what this great body of water would have to share. As I explored the coast I found a secluded beach and called upon the Spirit of the Water to see what would happen. A beautiful, feminine Being arose out of the ocean in my mind's eye. She held a very gentle energy as she spoke:

I am the Spirit of the Water. I am the Spirit of you Jane, for you are the water. You are the ocean. For you see, all life is given form through water – all life. It is the crystalline energy of creation – of manifestation. You can imbue your water with the request of what you choose to manifest. See it in the water, and then drink. This is powerful so be aware. Use only pure, non-manipulative energy in your request. For example, don't ask that so-and-so fall in love with you. That is interference. Instead request the pure knowing of love. How do you want it to feel? How will you behave in the presence of such love? What will you feel about yourself knowing this is love? This is the way to program your water.

Water is emotion – the ocean – (e)motion. Just as the tides are in constant motion, so too is the expression of feeling within the human. The ocean does not need to try and still itself as humans do, for the purpose of the water is to be your reflection. Have you noticed that water, when still, allows you to see yourself – your reflection? A diamond will sparkle and shine but it will not show you yourself. Only water will do this. So, as you look into the depths of the ocean know that what you see there is a reflection of your deepest feelings – what lies in the heart of humanity, for the water is a collection – a reflection of the collective you could say, just as humanity is a collective of each person on this planet.

As you know, your oceans are polluted. Your world is polluted. What lies without is created from within. What you see in your world and in your waters, is truly showing you what lies in the heart of humanity. It is no longer pristine. It has been corrupted. You need not blame yourselves for this corruption. It was placed beyond your control. And yet, you must claim your power and your intent to change it. The oceans, full of pollution and plastic from over-consumption, are a reflection of this corruption.

The waters are easily purified with human intention. Did you know this? Did you know how easily you can change the Earth and end the corruption? It is as easy as a song. Why do you think the beach is so soothing? Part of it is the rhythm of the waves and the sound. Part of it is the ionic composition of the air and part of it is a deep knowing, little recognized, of the power of water to transform. Just as tears transform your emotions and allow you to release, the oceans are a breathing, living system of the Earth. They are like the lungs of mother Earth – purifying, filtering, transforming the waters that are the source of life.

The more you begin to care for the land – the Earth – oceans included, the more you will be caring for yourselves. You will become softer. You can see the harshness of the world. There are sensitives now who cannot cope with it. There are not more mentally disturbed people on your Earth now, there are just more sensitive people who are revealing the insanity that has been existing on your planet for far too long. It has passed many cycles where it was meant to end. Now, in this new millennium, it appears humanity will be successful.

The ocean is one part of a living system that is Earth. Humanity, as a whole, is another part. The world is here as an Earth school. Therefore, what you contribute is what you see as your life's creation. You cannot change another but you can change yourself. Change how you are in the world. Change how you care about the world. The world needs more heart. What is it that determines the end of a human life? It is when the heart stops beating (aside from medical intervention). The oceans are like the heart of the Earth. When they become clogged they no longer support life. They reflect your empty hearts. Find love again Dear Humans.

Just like the trees, this beautiful water Being was inviting us back to love. Another thing about this message intrigued me. First was the mention of all life given form through water. Of course, we know that our bodies are made up of a large percentage of water. Still, I was inclined to do a little more research. According to the U. S. Geological Survey's Water Science School, "Water is of major importance to all living things; in some organisms, up to 90% of their body weight comes from water." That certainly would imply that the form of that organism is indeed created largely by water. The site goes on to say, "According to H.H. Mitchell, Journal of Biological Chemistry 158, the brain and heart are composed of 73% water, and the lungs are about 83% water." This could be why the ocean was referred to as the lungs of the Earth. Even though we know the purpose of our lungs is for breathing air, their composition is mostly water. That surprised me. As I was receiving the message, I had a vision of the oceans rising and sinking, like our lungs do as we breathe. I saw it as one massive movement as the entire ocean 'breathed'.[12] A few days after receiving this first message from the Pacific I went back to get more clarity about healing the water. Could it really be as simple as a song? I was curious as to what that meant. However, this time there was a different Being that wanted to present itself to me. She announced herself as Portia of the Pacific. She is of the elemental kingdom. Her role is similar to that of the human resources department in a corporation, only hers is for the elemental kingdom in relation to this ocean. She manages the tasks of the elemental kingdom in the role of maintaining the water and keeping it 'alive'. Here is what she shared with me:

Elementals are like nurse maids for nature. If there is an epidemic, a nurse cannot prevent someone from getting sick but s/he can make the recovery more comfortable and use her wisdom to aid in healing. So it is for the elementals of the Earth. We cannot prevent plastic from entering the ocean but we can support sea life to the best of our ability, to overcome it. We sometimes are the guides that lead sea creatures to humans to remove plastic from a turtle shell for example. Similar to humans having angels or Guides watching over them. We are this for life. My role is in the Pacific Ocean.

Humanity can be restored to love through water. As you have learned, water is emotion. Much of the demise of humanity is the dismissal of emotion while still having emotions. That is, you have judged your emotions as bad or unbalanced and you have not been taught how to manage your emotions. The process leads to suppression instead of expression. The suppression leads to anger expressed as aggression and hatred or inverted back to the self as self-loathing or denial. All of this has created a society that is unbalanced, unhealthy and unhappy.

In truth, the emotions of the human are your power. You feel for another and have compassion. You feel your own body responses, triggered by emotion, and have more understanding of your situation. Your emotions are your guiding system and your creative force. That knowledge has been manipulated to disempower you. Now is the time to claim your birth right to be whole and empowered and magnificent. You must claim it. No one is going to run up to you with this on a platter and coax you into accepting it. The choice is yours. It is the knowing of what you can choose that we offer here.

We see your ecological systems about to crash so it is our desire that you soon begin to step into your place once again as people of power. What is broken is obvious. Just look to nature to see the imbalance. The solution is also obvious. Look to the systems in nature that support one another and you will find it. Humans do not hold the only intelligence in the world. Nature itself is intelligence. You may want to consider that, and your connection to it, in your return back to empowerment.

As someone who is highly emotional, that is to say, I feel deeply, and who has been criticized in my life for being 'so sensitive', I can agree with what Portia has said. I would not trade my sensitive nature for anything. I know that I feel on a much deeper level than many people do. Interestingly, my emotional make-up comes from having many water elements in my astrology chart. That means that no doubt the pain goes deeper, and so does the love that I feel from the trees, and my Guides, and being in nature. Of course, the painful emotions come from humanity as we are still searching for love. It does not come from hanging out in the woods! That's when our emotions – our feelings - become a radar for what we are experiencing. In the dismissal of our emotions, we are taught to ignore that radar. Take the example of a young child who is taught to hug Uncle Willy because he is family, even when the child doesn't want to do so. Essentially, that child is being taught to override his natural feeling intelligence and replace it with mind logic. In the process of such conditioning we lose our intuitive, animal nature and instead begin to rationalize away what can be potentially harmful situations. If we were working on our emotional nature and allowing our instincts to guide us more freely there may be less people staying in abusive relationships or disregarding the small inner voice that says don't walk down that street tonight. Instead we use our rational, thinking minds to dismiss our more instinctual intuitive nature that holds great intelligence. It is heart intelligence. A beautiful base of operation if you ask me.

There is another level to this emotional radar that is awakening within me more all the time. I will sometimes get an uncomfortable feeling in my solar plexus when I am about to do something, or I am reading or watching something. The same feeling often comes up when I am doing clearing work. The solar plexus is connected to the subconscious and also often signals fear energy being released. It is a clear signal to me that what I am doing, or about to do, is not in my highest good. The more refined it becomes, the more it can relate to something that could easily be dismissed as insignificant. For example, I can be relaxing, reading a magazine, and I will get an uneasy feeling in my solar plexus or gut. It may a sign that it is time to get back to what I had committed to doing that day, or to be moving my body for some reason. It may even be something in the article that will not serve my highest good. The more I listen and respect it, the clearer it becomes. I feel like my body's language is becoming so fine tuned that, on days when I am completely in harmony with myself, every activity is directed by a higher aspect of who I am. Feelings redirect me when I am even slightly off track. These body intuitive nudges (which could be felt as emotions), I believe, come from a higher intelligence – my own Higher Self. I welcome such guidance in my life, especially knowing from HeartMath Institute research that our inner wisdom (intuition) reads a situation seconds before our logical mind does. Part of this may also stem from my daily intention to be living my greatest potential in every moment. Having that intention may be guiding me to things I'm not even aware of, and keeping me in the direction of the best outcome for my life.

After receiving this message from Portia, I went back to connecting with the beautiful, feminine Being that had arisen from the ocean a few days earlier. I wanted to go back to her statement that we can purify water and it is "as easy as a song." Years ago I worked with water and sound, which I will tell you about after I share what this watery Being revealed to me.

When a human sings to the water s/he is creating; therefore consider your song. Do not sing the blues. You can make up a song of whatever you desire. If you are singing to heal the ocean, you may praise it for its purity, its colour, its clarity. You may praise it for sustaining beautiful coral reefs and all life that exists around those reefs. You may thank it for sustaining life all over the planet with the process of evaporation and the cycles that water goes through. You can heal the waters this way by singing, out loud of course. You can make up the song. It need not rhyme or sound good to your ears. It is the process of speaking through song that creates. You must be clear in your intention and your visualization as you sing.

You may use this same principle in your life. You may sing a song to your drinking water for that which you desire. In this case, your song could be something like, "Thank you beautiful water, for holding the structure of joy in my life. I see you now transforming. I see you changing and so I change with you - for I am you. I Am the water that is joy. Joy is my creation. Joy is my essence through you." As you sing, visualize what joy feels like to you. Perhaps see yourself spinning, arms reaching to the heavens, in gratitude as you sing to your water.

This, Beloveds, can change your world. Sing to the seas as brimming with life — full of fish. See crystal, clear turquoise and blue waters. See plastic being sucked up by some great invention that cleans your oceans like a vacuum and then sing it as you imagine yourself at the beach or on a boat. This is the power of your imagination and song. This is the power of love — humans who know who they are. This is the beginning of your new world. The more of you who embrace it — who play with it and who will consider that there may be some truth here, the more you will see beneficial change in the world.

Again, I see deep truth in this message. Earlier in the book, I mentioned the work of Dr. Emoto of Japan who found a way to take pictures of water molecules. With his work he proved that water holds our intention and is influenced by prayers and pure intent. It is also negatively influenced by loud, angry music. In his book, Emoto shows water from the same source that was exposed to the words 'you fool' and 'I love you'. The 'you fool' water photo looked like an ugly blob as opposed to the 'I love you' exposure which formulated a beautiful crystal, like a snow flake. More recently, scientists in Germany have shown that water holds a different structure related to the people who are interacting with it. They conducted experiments with different people putting drops of water onto a slide to be examined under a microscope. Each person put their drops of water onto the slide at the same time from the same water source. What they found was that each person's slide would have a different signature you could say, that showed up in the water. Every drop created by the same person would have the same signature but it would be very different from another person's drop of water on a separate slide. Essentially, it looked like each person had created a different snow flake from the water. This tells me that water is not only influenced by our thoughts, but by our very presence. This is in alignment with quantum physics and our effect on the field. It takes me back to some of the messages in this book about the miracle that the air that we breathe has been the first breath of a newborn child. Similarly, the water we drink may hold the memories of many different events before it makes its way to our lips. That is reason enough to program it with our own highest thoughts and intentions![13]

When I first heard of the work of Dr. Emoto, I was in the practice of meditating daily and experimenting with sound. Most of the sound I was using at the time is what I have been guided to call Songs of Light. It is intuitive toning you could say. I would just open my mouth and allow whatever sound I was 'hearing' in my mind to come out. At least I would attempt to duplicate the sound! I had been playing with this for a few years before first learning about Dr. Emoto's work back in 2003. A few days after discovering that water holds human intention or prayer, I was inspired to create Rashana Sound Essences. I toned to the water, knowing that it would hold the intention behind the toning. In meditation I was guided to create ten different Rashana Sound Essences for emotional support. My favourite was Gratitude. When taking it daily I would experience deep washes of gratitude coming over me, for the smallest of things. I used to joke that I had gratitude in a bottle.

To test the effectiveness of the sound essences, I spent a year asking people to try them and offer feedback. Everyone felt the effects. Some were surprised at the shifts they felt within themselves. I remember one friend who was a bit insulted that I had been guided to give her 'Security' to try. She didn't think she needed security in her life. However, after using it for a week, she told me that she realized it was the perfect essence for her. She also told me that her teenage daughter was using it and found it gave her more self-confidence. Everyone who tried them had some experience to share. The reason I am telling you this is to validate that, being made mostly of water, when we sing to our water, or place intention in the water, it truly can change our experience. I invite you to do some research on Dr. Emoto and the changes he saw in the structure of the water with his experiments. You may feel inspired to do your own experiments with water. I would tone to the water to make my essences, yet toning is not the only way. You can sing to it and trust that the intention behind your words and your thoughts as you are directing it to the water that you will drink, will indeed make a difference. The energetic structure of the water changes with your song or intention and then, when you drink it, the energy creates a subtle change to the water in your body. It is similar to homeopathic healing which has been around since the 1800s. Homeopathy works on the principle that the more diluted the substance is, the greater effect it has on the body. Subtle energy moves past the physical to impact the deeper emotional level of our bodies. In this way, it is very gentle healing that works on all aspects of our energetic make-up and not just the physical body. Our mental, emotional and spiritual bodies are benefitting as well.

As I write, once again, I am having the synchronistic experience of information coming to me that supports the information being shared. Minutes after writing about water, and the impact of what we speak to the water, I was on FaceBook and someone had posted an article about songs that birds sing to their eggs before hatching and the influence it has on the young bird once it breaks free. The study was done with zebra finches in the wild. One scientist, who had been studying the birds for some time, discovered that, at times, the finches would sing a different song to the eggs in the nest during the last few days before hatching. This would happen when the weather was particularly hot. They found that the hatchlings, after being exposed to these specific hot weather songs, would be smaller in weight and remain so into adulthood. The baby finches that received the particular song would also prefer a warmer nesting area once they were mating. The scientists speculate that the birds prepare their young for a warmer climate based on the weather days before the eggs are expected to hatch. By remaining smaller in size, they believe the birds are better able to cope with the heat. I share this with you now to emphasize the power of sound and also the continual learning about the mystery of life. There is so much we don't know! Just as the ocean suggested we sing to change the water, we are learning that birds sing to change the development of their hatchlings. It's quite incredible to discover that the song a bird sings has such a powerful effect on the growing embryo, particularly at such a late stage of development.[14]

With water as the basis for all life, perhaps we should give more consideration to our ability to program it for healing within ourselves and for the Earth. I am becoming more and more aware of my thoughts and the words I speak with this knowledge. My body is listening. With this understanding I am also more particular about what I listen to and what songs I sing along with. The Rolling Stones' hit 'I Can't Get no Satisfaction' has a great beat and it's tempting to join in, but that beat is also a powerful influence on the subconscious. Now if I am listening to the radio and that song happens to come on, I change the words. Instead of "I can't get no satisfaction" I sing "Life is full of satisfaction … and I'm fine, and I'm fine …" It would be easy to dismiss the suggestion that we sing to our water to make change in our lives in part because it seems so simple. I believe that as complicated as the systems of nature are, the paradox is that it is also simple. Perhaps that's the true beauty - the system is so complicated and brilliant that it makes our lives simple (if we are not busy complicating it with our intellect).

In our expansion into a new level of awareness, we may come to understand that all of nature is here to support us, not just the trees. Even insects have something to teach us when we accept that everything happening in the outer world is showing us something about our inner world. I find myself embracing that knowing more and more. Some days I am so in tune with it that I notice every small detail as offering some guidance or awareness. In that, I understand that it is not *only* for me. Each person who comes into my experience is also learning from me as I mirror for them something about their inner world. It is part of the connection. We zip through each other's lives, mostly unaware of the significance of our interactions. I first discovered this when I started practicing the healing method I created – the

Freedom Release Technique. It soon became obvious that every person who came to me for support was showing me something within myself that was ready to be revealed and healed. Their expression in the outer world was a mirror for my inner world and vice-versa.

This same mirroring recently came to me from an experience with wasps. Not long after moving into my new home in Victoria I noticed wasps coming and going quite steadily outside my living room window. When I investigated I saw that they were going into the old pulley system that allows the windows to open and close. The house is over 100 years old, with single pane windows. I love the charm of the place, but soon discovered that the pulley system not only was accessible to the wasps from the outside. After about a week I noticed two or three wasps buzzing around on the inside. Now they really had my attention! It didn't take me long to discover that the metal wheel for the pulley system was connected to the inside, giving them an open door to my home, so-to-speak. Action was now required! I called my landlord, concerned not only about destroying the nest (which I felt terrible about) but also my health, not wanting chemicals used to kill the hive to come into my home through the same route as the wasps.

It was interesting that the wasps weren't aggressive at all. I wasn't comfortable with them coming into the apartment of course, yet never felt the threat of perhaps being stung by one of the wasps coming and going outside the window. Since it was a Friday evening before I heard back from my landlord, he informed me that it was going to have to wait until Monday for him to contact someone. I mustered up my courage that night, after the wasps had settled down somewhat, to tape up the pulley system on the inside and prevent any more getting in while I waited for the nest to be destroyed. In the meantime, I went online to look up the animal medicine of wasps – that is, to learn what the wasps were here to teach me. After all, this little insect was definitely in my reality. The first site I read talked about Feminine Warrior energy and productivity. Another site stated that wasps represent evolution and control over our life circumstances. All of that seemed to relate to my life situation at the time. However, the real message that wasp had for me was yet to come.

Monday morning the 'green' pest control company arrived. He told me he would use diatomaceous earth to take care of the nest. I was very grateful for this harmless manner of destroying the wasps. Apparently, the earth dries them out by pulling moisture out of their bodies as they crawl through it. He told me that the only problem would be if the queen survived. She would just start a new nest all over again. I felt very sad about the whole idea of killing the wasps that I knew were there to show me something. The burden of attracting them for what I knew to be a personal lesson, only to kill them, was weighing heavy on my heart. My feelings were no doubt magnified because it was happening at a time when I felt very vulnerable. I was being broken down as the planetary alignments of the time were squeezing the deep, dark vestiges of pain from my very being. I had just moved for the fourth time in twelve months to a community where I knew no one. Adding to that, the energies of transformation were upon me and I knew I was shifting and changing. What I went through in that time period was the deepest death/rebirth I have ever experienced. The wasps, as you will read, were reflecting that to me. After a couple of hours with diatomaceous earth in the nest, the activity had stopped. No wasps were visible and yet, their teaching continued.

The following day I was still thinking (and feeling guilty) about the wasps and feeling the deep emotions that were coursing through me. After making supper I decided to eat in the living room that I had been sitting in most of the afternoon. When I returned there, my eyes were drawn to the floor in the center of the room only to see a dead wasp! How it got there I do not know. The inside of the pulley wheel was still taped up and I hadn't seen any activity from the nest all day. I truly felt like the universe had placed it there so I would really get what they were showing me. I kneeled on the floor in front of the wasp, filled with sadness, for what I didn't even know, as some outside force was breaking down the me that I always knew. Tears were streaming down my face as I said, "Okay wasp spirit, show me everything you want me to know about this experience so I don't have to repeat it." Immediately I was shown how the queen fulfills her role. There was no sense of her feeling like royalty, placing herself above all others saying "serve me". No. The queen recognizes that she is of service to the whole nest. She recognizes the importance of her role and therefore the importance of those who serve her in their role. It is the Divine Plan. The workers serve her because she needs that support to fulfill her role, each serving the larger community.

As this awareness streamed into my mind, I realized that it was telling me of my role in the world. I have lived my life with a false sense of humility and what I call 'spiritual ego'. I misunderstood my belief that we are all deserving, to mean that we are all equal. We are not. We are all equally important, but we are not all equal. We each have a different role to play in service to All. In my vulnerable state that had brought me to my knees, I was open enough to see this truth. All my life I had focused on fairness and equality. In my opinion, a person is worthy not because of their position in the world, but because of their character. Somehow this had kept me from fully expressing my purpose in life and stepping into the greatness that I have come to share with the world. Now I can use that word greatness because of what wasp taught me. Stepping into my magnificence and being willing to step out and say 'here I am' is not putting myself above anyone or believing I am better than anyone. It is none-the-less powerful in declaring and claiming the fullness of who I am and stepping out of playing small to avoid offending others who are not ready to claim that for themselves. It was a great lesson for me.

With this new awareness, wasp had one more thing to show me. A couple of days after finding the dead wasp on the floor, which I had assumed was the queen, I heard that buzzing sound on my window again. At first I thought it must have been outside. Then, I heard it again and sure enough, there was a wasp inside my window! This one had longer antennae that curled at the end and it was larger than the others. It seemed that the queen had indeed survived and she revealed herself to me so that I might complete my learning! This time I had to take care of the wasp myself and I knew there was significance in that. I had to be empowered and catch the queen and destroy her so that she wouldn't nest again in the same spot. I caught her with a glass jar and poured in some diatomaceous Earth to be sure that she would not survive. This time I had shifted. I was not sad. To the contrary, I felt good about taking charge of my life situation. A strength was emerging from within after allowing myself to be swallowed up by the spiritual death that was happening days before. In the two weeks following that whole scenario, I found myself birthed into a completely new awareness of living more fully in the world. I am not the same person I had been. I transformed out of a dream state of living on hope, and imagined projections of what 'might' be, into being fully anchored in reality. With it came a true sense of taking care of myself and a new perspective of being, for the first time in my life, fully present in the physical world. I know my mission now, like the queen wasp, to live my purpose and allow others to support me along the way, all contributing to the wholeness that honours all life.

I share my wasp story with you so that you can see the interconnection between all things – all life upon this planet. My old mantra, all change leads to something better, is no longer required. In its place is a maturity and a knowing that *I* am the change that leads to something better. That 'change' has come from releasing many layers of pain and suffering that have been my human journey. My burden led me to be a warrior in my life, holding the suffering for so long that I didn't know how to soften and allow the cure – love of self. It is a human condition. For me the change started by dedicating the year 2012 to healing. Many years later I am still peeling off layers to reveal the magnificence of my true self. I am becoming a new human on this new Earth, not so much by changing who I am, although it would appear that way. It's more like a Russian nesting doll, removing all the layers of who I am not, as I work back to my true essence. Life is stripping away all the protective layers that I created as a shield from the harsh reality of a 3D world to reveal my true self, hidden deep within the walls of layer after layer of defense. The more this awakens, the more I feel a heart-felt pull toward my fellow man.

Being over 60 years old, I am amused that the little child within has finally grown up - not with the passing of years but with the removal of the debris that had her frightened and withdrawn. Only when the world is a safe place to be can we reveal our deepest truth – our greatest brilliance. For too long we have been suppressed because of our radiance. Now is the time to burst through the layers of suppression and be the fullest expression of our human magnificence. My beautiful teachers, the trees, have led me here. Even coming to Vancouver Island, where I was completely broken apart within a month, was led by the trees. And I thank them, for without my crumbling I may still be searching for myself.

My journey will continue, for it is a never-ending quest to know love. By returning to source through nature I am coming to know that love. I have felt the unconditional acceptance that comes from the trees. I have wept with the gift of sunlight gracing the forest floor in wisps of dancing light. I have spun with the wind as it reminded me that I am alive, in a pulsing rhythm of intelligence. I am returning to wholeness. I am returning to the great creation that is human on this most sacred planet Earth. As my love awakens for all the natural world around me, it awakens for myself. That is the invitation. That is the new human on a new Earth. We are of one source. When I connect with a tree I am connecting with my own soul. Its wisdom is my wisdom, filtering to me through the great intelligence that has me believing that I am separate. It has worked for a long, long time. And now I can awaken – awaken to the ever-expanding Light that is all life.

It is safe to awaken to love. That is what the trees want us to know. They have more love for us than we have for ourselves it seems. Thankfully so. As we witness ourselves through their love, we will heal. In our healing, we will honour each other and all of creation. In that honouring we will find ourselves living in a new world – a world full of Love Existing. Come join me there.

Correspondence

Please email any inquiries or questions to info@conversationswithatree.com.

Visit www.conversationswithatree.com to purchase additional copies of the book. Join our mailing list to receive free monthly tree messages and stay informed of activities and events related to this book.

Our FaceBook page is
https://www.facebook.com/conversationswithatree/

I have several meditations and more recently, tree related videos, on my YouTube channel
http://www.youtube.com/user/Rashana88

Acknowledgments

I would like to thank Claire Gerus for her curiosity about *Conversations with a Tree* that led to this edition, and her invaluable insights about what would make the book worth reading. Without you it never would have happened. To my many dear friends, who took the time to read the book and offer their insights, I am deeply grateful. My heart-felt thanks to Terry Choyce who first encouraged me to step into my potential by setting up invitations for me to speak and share my work. It is by doing that we learn. And, my deepest thanks goes to the tree Henrietta for inviting me into the world of wisdom and guidance that only she could offer.

Thanks to Kjpargeter - Freepik.com for creating the beautiful cover image and to the staff at BookClaw for the cover design and formatting of this book.

About the Author

Jane Warren Campbell (aka. Rashana) lives on Vancouver Island, Canada. She is an author, speaker, Earth Walk facilitator, and intuitive Nature Communicator. Her interest in alternative therapies, and her personal healing journey, led to the creation of the Freedom Release Technique, Rashana Sound Essences and Tree Spirit Essences. Jane has written two children's books and *Conversations with a Tree* is her third adult book (all available on her website).

www.conversationswithatree.com
www.rashana.ca
www.freedomreleasetechnique.com
www.treespiritessences.com

References

[1] linv.org/wp-content/uploads/2014/10/054-macleans

[2] http://www.theguardian.com/environment/radical-conservation/2015/aug/04/plants-intelligent-sentient-book-brilliant-green-internet

[3] http://news.nationalgeographic.com/2016/02/160221-plant-science-botany-evolution-mabey-ngbooktalk/

[4] linv.org/wp-content/uploads/2014/10/054-macleans

[5] linv.org/wp-content/uploads/2014/10/054-macleans

[6] https://www.youtube.com/watch?v=vU6yCD_sEvU

[7] http://www.hphpcentral.com/article/forest-bathing

[8] p. 51 *Last Child in the Woods*

[9] http://www.outsideonline.com/1870381/take-two-hours-pine-forest-and-call-me-morning

[10] http://www.healinglandscapes.org/blog/2011/01/its-in-the-dirt-bacteria-in-soil-makes-us-happier-smarter/

[11] http://www.universetoday.com/121930/more-evidence-that-comets-may-have-brought-life-to-earth/

[12] http://water.usgs.gov/edu/propertyyou.html

[13] http://www.lifebuzz.com/water-theory/

[14] http://www.smithsonianmag.com/science-nature/birds-talk-their-eggsand-song-might-help-their-babies-deal-climate-change-180960168/?no-ist

Manufactured by Amazon.ca
Bolton, ON